The
Door of
Everything

by

RUBY NELSON

DeVorss & Co., *Publishers*
P.O. Box 550
Marina Del Rey, Ca. 90294

ISBN: 0-87516-069-7

Printed in the United States of America

CONTENTS

Part One: *The Vision*

1   *The Father Consciousness* 11

2   *The Sub-Creation* 22

3   *Grand Cosmic Being* 35

4   *The Sacred Seed* 55

5   *The Holy Spirit* 68

6   *The Second Birth* 85

Part Two: *Living Upward*

7   *The Ascension Attitudes* 103

8   *The Supporting Attitudes* 129

9   *The Mighty Rock* 136

10 *The Total Stillness* 149

11 *The Lightning Flash* 164

12 *The Door of Everything* 176

PART ONE:

THE VISION

"I was crowned by my God, my crown is
     living . . .

I received the face and the fashion of
     a new person . . .

And the thought of truth led me on.

I walked after it and did not wander.

And all that have seen me were amazed
     and I was regarded by them
     as a strange person.

And He who knew and brought me up is
     the Most High in all His
     perfection. And He glorified
     me by His kindness, and raised
     my thoughts to the height of
     His truth.

And from thence He gave me the way of
     His precepts and I opened the
     doors that were closed.

And broke in pieces the bars of iron;
     but my iron melted and dissolved
     before me:

Nothing appeared closed to me, because
     I was the door of everything."

—Odes of Solomon

The Father Consciousness

CHAPTER 1

Walk with me, the guiding voice of Father consciousness at the center of your soul, and I will lead you gently onward and raise your thoughts to the height of truth.

I am the Light of Life within you and I have continued to shine through all the darkness of your manifold experiences, but your darkness has comprehended me not.

I am also the Light of the world and the power thereof by which it was made. Contrary to appearances, I am not a lazy God who created the world and rested, then kept right on resting, indifferent to the fate of the many souls

I made. The truth is that I am always with you, no matter where you are, for in me you live and move and have your being.

If you would become conscious of my presence, look squarely in my face; stretch your mind and heart and take a long, thorough, independent look. I will be everywhere staring boldly back at you. If you look at the sky you will know that I am blue, if you look at the night you will know that I am black, if you look at a leaf you will know that I am green. If you look at the midday sun I will dazzle you with my brightness. If you look into the eyes of your husband or wife, you will see me twinkle.

If you look at the ground on which you stand, you will know that it is holy. Every particle of dirt under your feet is a manifestation of my consciousness expressing in matter, and in the microcosmic structure of this dirt exists the unchallenged pattern of my universal perfection. If you could behold these particles of dirt with extended vision, you would see that they are vibrant with my eternal Light.

This radiant Light of my presence is in all things, from the lowly weeds to the stately trees to the most opulent galaxies, far-flung in space. The kitten curled up in your lap is as much a part of me as the baby on your knee, and whatever you do to the least of one of these you do also unto me.

Normally, you may not think of me when you behold such commonplace things as weeds or trees or babies. You are more likely to think of me when telescopes peer into the depths of my unbounded cosmos and bring back news of the awe-inspiring reaches of stars and galaxies and cosmic clouds, or when you hear mysterious mumblings about other dimensions, other realms. A baby, you say, or weed or tree is just something formed from the dust of earth. And what is this dust of earth except a part of that awe-inspiring cosmos which just reminded you of me? Is there anything less awe-inspiring about a baby than about a galaxy, excluding, of course, the difference in size? Perhaps, if size were to be a consideration, the baby would be the most awe-inspiring because so much of my Light has been contained in such a compact bundle.

When you have felt lost and desperate, yearning for a sign from me, you were surrounded by exquisite signs of beauty, growth and color, and you recognized them not as being mine. True, my form is familiar to you, you have seen it every day. I built your world out of my own Spirit and filled it with my all-pervading presence so you would know indisputably that in me you live and move and have your being.

And in you I live and move and have *my* being.

In a thousand different places you keep searching for me, finding tidbits of information about me everywhere you look, though most of it turns out to be intangible and incomplete, failing to show the way to firsthand consciousness of my presence. Nevertheless, the restlessness in your soul motivates you to keep the search continuing; deep beneath your heart is the tantalizing sureness that Oneness with me can be found. Yet I seem ever to elude, to stay just beyond reach, to lure you onward for a time and then desert you in some cul-de-sac of confusion and frustration.

All the while, I am so close to you I have been overlooked, you have taken me for granted until you no longer recognize me. As you reach outward hoping to find me, I hide in your mind, your heart, your soul, I hide in the consciousness within you.

For I am your well of living waters, your reservoir of life force, and if you will learn to draw from my resources, eagerly and deliberately, these resources will increase and multiply until your entire being is transformed into a vessel unceasingly running over with holy radiance.

My presence as your inner consciousness is just as infinite as my unending presence in the cosmos all around you.

Like an iceberg on the sea, nine-tenths of which is out of sight, I live within you in the form of mind with nine-tenths of me being submerged beneath your awareness. The expanse of an iceberg underwater is just as real as the tip extending above the surface. And the expanse of mind submerged below your conscious awareness is just as real as the surface mind with which you do your thinking.

The submerged mind is like a sunken treasure chest, chock-full of wonders, waiting for you to discover it and draw it to the surface. For the most part, it lies neglected and untouched even though I have stored within it all my powers, all my wisdom, all the truth in the cosmos, the record of existence, the force that quickens and perfects, the peace that passes understanding, the love that conquers all.

This submerged mind is your center of divine wisdom, an area of mind that does not think in the normal sense of the word—it knows. The nature of it is pure and holy, it has never been touched by limited or negative belief; it is a living part of me. When you have learned to elevate this submerged mind and integrate it with your surface consciousness, your entire being will take on its holy nature and you will come to find

that, as Jesus taught, it is indeed not
robbery to be equal with God.

Your submerged mind extends into the
central area of feeling, the heart. I live
also in your heart as a reservoir of love
that is immeasurable. Your hopes and
dreams and high aspirations rise up from
this reservoir of feeling; they are the
echoes of my still small voice, bursting
through to your surface mind like notes
of music springing out of the silence, forever urging you onward toward more
prolific expression of your hidden skills
and talents.

Unfortunately, however, much more
than hopes and dreams and high aspirations has been born in your central reservoir of feeling. For mind and heart
have always worked together to form a
powerful force. When thought combines
with feeling, activity is set in motion,
things are brought about. The more in-

tense the feeling, the greater is its active force.

It is for this one reason, simple though it may sound, that the many kinds of troubles which plague the world have been brought into existence.

My children have misused their thoughts, they have misused their feelings; innocently doing so, of course, not knowing of the mighty forces set in motion when thoughts and feelings blend.

It is because of this misuse of thought and feeling that my planet earth has been perverted. In actuality, it is a perfect world which I prepared with tender care and filled abundantly with my presence. However, since thoughts and feelings are living forces, and my children have let their thinking sink to imperfect levels, imperfect conditions are in operation, abounding and rebounding, superimposed, as it were, over my beautiful planet like a sinister spiderweb.

This superimposed web of destructive forces is merely the sub-creation of the surface mind, that strictly-human side of mind which evolved away from the Father consciousness and left my treasure chest of wisdom beneath the level of awareness.

Jesus called this web of sub-creation "appearances." Knowing that it lacked a foundation in Reality, he taught the people of the world not to judge by appearances. He knew the power of the sub-creation was none other than the power which surface minds were giving it by belief in negative conditions and fear of destructive forces.

He knew also of that submerged center of divine omniscience which is a living part of every soul on earth. He called this center the Father consciousness and taught that He who is within you is stronger than any power without. The creative power of thought and feeling originating in the submerged mind is ten thousand times as great as the creative power of thought and feeling originating in the surface mind.

For this reason, the destructive forces running rampant in the sub-creation can be overcome by anyone who learns the truth of how to integrate the surface mind with the holy Father consciousness.

When I created you in my image and likeness, I made you perfect and placed you in a perfect world. I gave you a mind which is Whole, it is One with me. Within that one mind, however, are many rates of vibration, resulting in many levels of consciousness.

At the summit of the highest level of human consciousness there is a "Door" through which you can slip and be free from all the influences you are under in the sub-creation.

The Sub-Creation

CHAPTER 2

To call the web of human sub-creation "appearances" is not to say that it is imaginary. Actually, it is real, painfully — sometimes inhumanly — real and active. Within this web of collective forces are included many experiences which have been accepted as the way life is—wars, conflicts, violence, strife and troubles in any form, poverty, disease, old age, the cycles of death and rebirth, the struggle of mankind to understand himself and his universe.

Since such imperfections have generally been accepted without question, very few of my lost children have tried to find perfection by coming to realize that

I have already given to each and every one a mind that knows all things and has all power, and a life force which cannot age since it is the essence of eternal youth.

Instead of reaching this point of realization, some of my children think I have thrown them into the searing earthly experiences so they can learn to face troubles and live with them. Some think it is my way of punishing them for past sins. Others think the reason for it all is that I am attempting to form perfect beings by slow trial-and-error methods, shaping a little here, rounding a little there, filing off somewhere else, a process which is supposed to go on for thousands of lifetimes while each is being honed down to the essence I want. Still others believe that I am testing to see if they are worthy to inherit heaven after death. If found unworthy, the belief goes, satan will inherit the soul and it will be tormented forever in a lake of fire and brimstone.

All of these stories are products of the surface mind, misinterpretations of my Word. Jesus came to earth to set men free from such beliefs, to let my children know that as they think in their hearts, so are they.

How do you think "in your heart"? Is that not the area of deep feeling commonly known as the subconscious mind which is fully conditioned by past happenings, by fears and doubts and unpleasant memories, by mixtures of the good as well as the bad, until most of your actions and reactions have become automatic habits? This "heart" is a very important center to understand.

It is like a vast reservoir constantly being filled with whatever you pour into it through the surface mind. The quality of the ideas in your personal reservoir determines the quality of your actions and reactions. If you have filled your reservoir with accepted human beliefs in limitation, then you are limited in all your actions. But if you are willing to empty out your heart and let me fill it with eternal truth, you will experience a transformation.

Your heart is your creative center. It is like a powerful dynamo transmuting the thoughts and emotions with which you fill it into manifested form. For instance, why is it that the things Job feared came upon him? He mulled his fears in his mind and they were so alive for him, so intense, they blended with his feelings and fell into the creative reservoir where they were transformed into the very substance of the image in his surface mind.

This creative endowment of your heart center is not a bizarre flaw in the way I made you. It was my intent that the desires of your heart should always be fulfilled. Through proper use of this creative reservoir, anything that the

Father has can be manifested in your own life, if you are persistent and your yearnings are intense.

However, since I created only perfection, I did not mean for you to fill your minds with images of evil, letting these evil images drop into the creative reservoir and come back to you manifested as outer forces over which you have no personal control.

Your ever-active heart center works on an automatic basis. It projects a "mold", as it were, into my uncreated spiritual elements, and this mold assumes the shape of whatever has been strongly visualized in the surface mind. The heart center does not screen out experiences and materialize only that which is good for you, since the surface mind itself is the screening master, and once an image has fallen into the feelings and been sustained there, the manifestation of the image perceived is automatic.

Therefore, an "emptying out" of your surface mind is essential to your ability to realize and experience the perfection of my cosmos. Since creativity is a continuous process, and I have made you in such a way that you can have anything you "feel" for, you can experience perfect Oneness with me just as readily as you have been experiencing an utter sense of separation from me.

The secret is to control the point at which your attention is focussed. All of my children are gods with creative powers similar to my own, and by controlling the point of conscious focus, the sub-creation can be erased just as easily as it was brought about.

It has never pleased me to have you suffer from the unpleasant experiences created by misthinking, and I have set up no rigid laws that say you must accept the consequences of your mistakes.

Instead, I have tried to tell you that

I forgive sins instantly, I cancel out the many effects of wrong-thinking, I pull you through that Door in mind and gather you under the shadow of my protective wing as soon as you stretch out your hand to let me know that you are ready.

If this were not true, Jesus would have been forced to turn away many trusting souls who came to him believing he could give them help. He probably would have said to Mary Magdalene something like this: "Sorry, Mary, but you really are a wanton woman. You will have to reap what you have sown sooner or later. Might as well let the stones hit you and get it over with."

Of course he said no such thing. Well he knew my eagerness and my power to cancel out all imperfect forces that are in operation. Well he knew that Mary was my beloved daughter and though her sins were as scarlet I waited to make her white as snow.

It is the same with you. You reap what you have sown as long as your surface mind is drifting here and there between the poles of good and evil, and your feelings are implanted by this surface mixture. As soon as you accept the truth of my eternal perfection and learn to master the surface mind, thereby controlling the reservoir of feeling, your level of consciousness is elevated to that transcendental apex wherein all evil conditions fall under the dominion of my Light.

It was on this high level of consciousness that Jesus lived, on the inside of that Door to submerged mind. From this exalted level, he was able to erase the appearances of the sub-creation and restore perfection to my ailing children. Not only did he overcome death of his own body, he restored the bodies of others who had died.

Lazarus was a very dear friend and Jesus taught him and Mary and Martha

my most precious truths. Lazarus could
have overcome death for himself if he
had accepted these truths thoroughly
enough to make them active in his creative dynamo of feeling. He was accepting
these teachings with his surface mind,
but they had not become subconscious, he
had not grasped the feeling of truth fully
enough for it to drop into the heart center and be manifested as the reality of
his experiences. His subconscious still
harbored the old belief that death and
the grave are necessary steps along the
road to eternity. Therefore, he died, as
do all who hold to this belief since there
is so much evidence in its favor. Jesus
wept because Lazarus was in possession
of the truth that makes men free from
earthly law, but he had been unable to
let go of the old long enough to put on
the new.

Lazarus was reaping what he had
sown in the subconscious; the earthly law

of cause-and-consequence had done its destructive work. Still, this did not stop Jesus. My power within is always greater than any power without. When Jesus said, "Lazarus, come forth," the law of cause-and-consequence was superseded and even the decaying body cells responded to his unspoken recognition of my omnipresent life.

When questioned once about a number of Galileans who had been destroyed, Jesus answered, "Suppose ye that these Galileans were sinners above all the Galileans because they suffered such things? I tell you, nay; but except ye repent, ye shall all likewise perish. Or those eighteen, upon whom the tower of Siloam fell, and slew them, think ye that they were sinners above all men that dwelt in Jerusalem? I tell you, nay; but except ye repent, ye shall all likewise perish."

Except you repent—except you turn around exactly where you are and swing your thoughts and feelings to the positive pole, sooner or later the wages of negative reactions will mean destruction for you too.

As soon as you refuse to be blinded by the web of sub-creation and cease using your mixed thought forces to sustain it, it will dissolve before you, first individually, then collectively, and you will be lifted free into the promised land of good.

Then you will see me as I am and know at last it never was my will to have you boiling in such a torrid earthly stewpot. You have always been willing to believe, have you not, in a God who has all wisdom and all power? Then why should you be deceived into thinking that I was unable to make you perfect when I created you? Had I to leave you half-finished, a fragile, defenseless creature, often incapable of dealing with the environment around you?

The truth is that I created you in my image and likeness, and you are destined to realize this equality in its fullest measure. The missing link in this realization has been the surface mind and its tendency to remain focussed in the wrong direction.

I stand at the Door of your consciousness, knocking. If you will only turn toward me, emptying yourself out to receive my Spirit, I will pour so much Light into the reservoir of your heart that it will run over with goodness and mercy all the days of your eternal life.

By the power of this Light your subconscious reservoir of feeling can be lifted up to its original purity, thereby exalting your reactions, causing you to put on the living crown of life, to receive the face and the fashion of a new person, to open the Door in consciousness which has been closed to you. When this happens the old order of life will pass away, the subcreated web which seemed as invincible as enclosing bars of iron will melt and dissolve before you. This renovation does not depend on time or place but solely on your acceptance and application of the truth that you are really created in the image and likeness of your God.

Grand Cosmic Being

CHAPTER 3

When I created you in my image and likeness, I endowed your being with the greatest gift I had to give. Alas! this greatest gift has seldom been received or understood.

For I so loved the world I gave my only begotten Son that whosoever believed in him would not perish but have everlasting life.

It is a generally accepted belief that Jesus was my only begotten Son. Some of you have been taught that if you believe Jesus was the only begotten of the Father, you will not perish, you will have everlasting life after you have died.

The real truth is that the only begot-

ten of the Father is a Grand Cosmic Being, a perfect man or woman, a radiant
image clothed in robes of shimmering
Light, a godlike ideal who claims the
cosmos for his playground and comes and
goes with the speed of thought, a joyous
being whose vibration is quickened to
the rate of mine and whose consciousness
is as expansive as mine — the Living
Christ.

Yes, I so loved the world and all my
children in it that I gave to each and
every one of you this most cherished
gift—I created you by the pattern of
the Living Christ. My only command to
you was that you believe it and live ac-
cordingly.

So simple, so easy. My image and likeness placed inside each and every one
as your nucleus, your very mind and soul,
and all you have to do is believe in your
own Self.

How much longer must I wait for you

to learn? Oh my children, all of you could join a mighty calvacade of majestic gods who even now are winging their way across the face of the deep singing a chorus of praise and joy, but you will not. Even though the Spirit and the bride say come, and he who hears could come, you will not. You are too busy with the mundane pastimes of earthly occupations to listen to the call.

If you should be still long enough to hear the call, you would most likely hesitate, doubting, thinking it is all too good to be true.

In spite of your doubts, that submerged mind of divine holiness is a living part of you; your polluted reservoir of feeling contains power enough to erect mountains; and my image is your identity for I am truly your Light of Life.

If you do not believe my words, try believing in the Grand Cosmic Being, try feeling Its identity inside you, and you will see for yourself.

That is what Jesus did, of course, and when you were instructed to let the same mind be in you which was also in Christ Jesus, you were not being told to try to develop this mind, or evolve it, or create it, but just to elevate it and let it express.

When Jesus learned that divine omniscience is the nucleus of everyone, he held his life in prayerful stillness till he was conscious of my presence, then took up residence with me and began to experience all wisdom, all love, all power.

There are no laws in existence to say you cannot do the same. In fact, my holy laws say that you can. And I am waiting, with arms outreaching, until you do.

I know there appears to be contradiction in my words. If Jesus claimed his identity as the Living Christ and became

a Grand Cosmic Being who knows all
things and has all power, why did he die
such a painful death on the cross? What
happened to the goodness and mercy
which I have promised to pour out on
all who turn to me? Who wants to realize
his Christhood when it appears to increase the dangers to be faced?

These are indeed worthy questions and
they deserve to be answered.

As you will readily agree, Jesus was
the greatest revealor of truth ever to live
on earth. Not that he has been the only
one; there have been thousands of others,
some in the present day, but he is
the supreme example. He made the
greatest sacrifice of all. He did it willingly, knowing what was coming, holding back his already-quickened vibration
to the mortal level and allowing it to
happen, all because of his great love for
you.

Yes, Jesus loves you even as I do in

spite of the fact that you are so hard to teach. The human side of mind is very reluctant to unlearn the old and reach out for the new, even when the new is the very thing for which it has been yearning.

If this were not so, then the sacrifice made by Jesus would not have been necessary. He would not have had to die at all. He could merely have told you that, through the grace of Holy Spirit, I expect you to be master over the elements, master over your body, in charge of every single cell so completely that you could resurrect it even though it were in a state of decay. No, it was necessary to show that this is possible, and Jesus went through it willingly to show the world.

In spite of his loving sacrifice, many have missed the message. Jesus was the Son of God, you say, a man of virgin birth, and that makes him different. You are a mere mortal born of flesh and you could never be expected to do the impossible sort of things that the Son of God has done. It furnishes a perfect excuse for not trying.

But you are letting the loving sacrifice of your greatest teacher go to waste. Each time you turn away and bother not to comprehend the example he set for all to follow, you are driving more nails into the cross, crucifying not him, but your own Self, over and over again.

For you are just as surely a Son of God as Jesus is, the soul in each of you is a living part of me. As soon as you let it stand forth in full expression, your body will be as indestructible as your greatest teacher's was. You can come and go like the wind and no one will know from whence or to whither, just as it was with Jesus, for your body will be transmuted into a fast-vibrating organism that can carry the high-potency of my Holy Spirit. And if you should choose

to make the sacrifice of death and resurrection to reveal the truth of everlasting
life, you will be richly rewarded. Such
a sacrifice, made to show the unbelieving
surface minds, will release so much love
within your soul that you could float a
solar system upon this love and still it
would keep gushing up and pouring out
into the deep.

While this sacrifice is being made by
you, the human mind with limited vision, judging from appearances, would
most likely be feeling pity that you had
come to such a bad end. The human
mind tends to emphasize the suffering,
pointing out how all the saints have suffered, being completely unaware that
man causes the suffering by his unwill-
ingness to believe. Also being unaware
that my Spirit is on hand, with a host
of heavenly angels, to lavishly bestow
rewards on one who makes a sacrifice
that others might receive a sign. We

leave the scene together, rejoicing in a job well done, firm in our knowledge that someday all mankind will see through appearances and behold my Light.

Already a new age of understanding is dawning upon my beautiful planet earth. Much superstition and false interpretation is falling by the wayside while many minds are moving upward toward a new level of consciousness wherein they no longer try to attack and **do harm to one who reveals my power.** They may ignore him and not recognize his words of truth because these words are so simple, but that reaction is a step forward, an elevation removed from the level of consciousness on which they approached him with violent intent.

The hardest task that the surface mind must face if it is to cooperate with my will is the task of unlearning ideas universally accepted as truth and taking on

such implausible ideas as belief in unlimited inner powers and eternal life for
all.

My unhappy earth children should be
delighted when they hear the good news
that the message of the Christ contains.
But some reject it, either because of fear
or doubt, or because a little too much
mental effort is required to push old
opinions out of consciousness. Nevertheless, it is these old beliefs in mixtures of
good and evil that have oppressed the
Christ spirit and kept you from being
exalted to my kingdom long ago. You
should be glad to let these threadbare
opinions fall away for the sake of something better. They are the same opinions,
with variations here and there, that have
been clung to, passed around, and handed down from generation to generation
without much added enlightenment.

The practice has been to accept whatever ideas you are exposed to, to accept

the ways of the ancestors, more or less, and question them not at all. This in spite of the fact that Jesus revealed the revolutionary pathway of independent thinking, the pathway of aligning your thought forces with the forces of creation. This is not the pathway of making up universal laws to suit yourself; it is the pathway of withdrawing from the race beliefs and aligning yourself with the onrushing River of Life More Abundant so that your inborn originality has its chance to express and eternally unfold.

History bears witness to the fact that few of your ancestors understood the message of eternal life. Why look to their methods, expecting these methods to benefit you any more than they benefitted them? Did they not fall together into the ditch of death toward which you are heading by following in their footsteps?

Withdrawal from race beliefs is the first important step if you wish to shift your center of consciousness to the inside of that Door in mind, the Door that leads into my kingdom, that opens up for you a garden paradise of Reality among the stars.

Imagine what a wonderful place the earth will be when all my children learn the truth about their relationship to me and begin to weave it into their every thought and act. Imagine how easily lives will change, how easily the dove of peace can spread her white wings and settle down over the planet. Behold, I make all things new, including your bodies, my holy temples, which will be transmuted into the invisible when they are filled with my Spirit. For this Spirit is potent and not one single organism can open to receive it and remain unchanged. Not one stone shall be unturned on that great day when my image and likeness is allowed to increase on earth.

Even now a few of you are beginning to know your Grand Cosmic Self. You have been introduced to Yourself as you studied the teachings of my Word. You have taken this unspeakable revelation into your reservoir of feeling, cherished it in golden silence, and guarded it from all dark forces while it began to grow toward maturity. And it has been an untouchable, indescribable thing, a glow in your interior, like a bright star caught inside some tunnel, and you have been unable to share it, knowing full well that it can never be reduced to the dullness of intellectual ideas.

But as you cherish this revelation, this Christ child of truth within you, you too will experience a virgin birth, and I will give you words with which to shout my glorious truth from the housetops of the world.

The juicy red tomato on your dinner table would never have appeared if a tomato seed had not been previously planted. The seed was planted, it was fertilized, it was watered, and then allowed to grow until the day of ripeness. After that, only a moment was needed to pick it.

The full realization of your true identity, your master pattern, does not suddenly burst upon you until the seed of truth has been planted, nourished, cherished, and allowed to mature to ripeness. This does not take thousands of years, it does not take hundreds, it may take only a few short years, a few months, a few weeks, depending entirely upon your attitude and intensity.

You understand, of course, that I am the one who does the work of fulfillment. I do not mean to imply that you are expected to metamorphose yourself through some superhuman determination. Your part is merely to show that you are willing to trust your future to me, willing to let my will be done, willing to align your purposes with mine through the comprehension of my Word and the quieting of your heart.

My Word grows vigorously in your consciousness once it gets a firm foothold. But it does need some care to keep it healthy. It needs to be watered with your faith lest it should wither and dry up, and it responds mightily when nourished with your prayers. However, as you continue to apply faith and prayer, you must be patient and leave the rest to me. A tomato does not receive its increase from the farmer who tends it. The increase comes from me. My truth inside you will grow and ripen, not by your power but by mine.

Until such time as you consciously and subconsciously accept the good news of the Christ, you will continue to be trapped in the web of sub-creation, traveling in a circle on a wheel of cause-and-consequence, confused by the mad whirling, too busy holding onto the flying spokes to see my hand above you, reaching toward you, ready to lift you off the wheel and set you free.

Each life I give you is a new opportunity, a second, third, and fourth chance, ad infinitum, to put your hand in mine and let me exalt your mind and body to that god-like level wherein you have dominion over all appearances.

My entire cosmos is made up in very orderly fashion. All my galaxies follow the same general pattern, though when you start to explore them you discover no two are alike in detail. All my suns are round, so to speak, none of them are square. All my microcosmic motions follow similar basic specifications.

The same divine perfection was intended for all my children. Within the pattern of your Being is contained your originality and your freedom to express it. But first you must show that you are willing to fulfill your Cosmic Selfhood and go purposefully about the business of your Father consciousness before you will experience this universal perfection. As long as you are intent only on the purposes of your human selfhood, the web of sub-creation will continue to grow up around you, blinding you to Reality.

When nothing matters to you except my will be done, I will know that you are ready to put your hand in mine, and I will lift you off the wheel, then come in and feast with you, filling your body with my fires of purification, dissolving all the sins in you as sunlight dissolves shadow, transmuting the cells from end to end of you into my perfect spiritual substance.

As long as you are taking thought for tomorrow, you have not reached the level of consciousness which wills only that my will be done. Concern for to-morrow, in any form, betrays the fact that you are still involved with the purposes of the human self. Concern for to-morrow also means that you do not trust me, you are still looking at the seeming-powers of the sub-creation and trying to worship duality. Keep your eye single to my glory with all the faith that you can muster. How can I trust you to be my Grand Cosmic Being if you will not trust me to be your helpful heavenly father?

Jesus relinquished himself completely to me that day on the cross. The per-sonality, the body, the desires of the sur-face mind, all were handed over to my will. His crucifixion symbolized the com-plete letting go of self which I must ask of all my children. For he who loses his life for my sake shall find it in his greater Selfhood.

Your surface personality is of little

worth in my kingdom since you are like the tomato seed, the personality being the hull which is needed no more as soon as the kernel is allowed to sprout.

This relinquishing of your surface self may take a lot of effort. It may be enough to keep you occupied for quite some time if you are a victim of deep-seated habit as are most of my earth children. But you will be richly rewarded if you can cast away old patterns of thought, old habits of doubt, and keep the image of yourself as the Living Christ in your mind's eye so strongly your focus never wanders and your subconscious feelings never falter in reacting in accordance with this truth.

There is no need to condemn yourself for being weak if old reactions creep in at first to make the task of habit-changing seem virtually impossible. Neither will I condemn you. Just remember that all things are possible to one who loves

God, and soon, as you try again, the
former manner of thinking will have
passed away, the Christ nature will be
seeping through into your surface mind,
and you will be quite naturally merging
into the high ideal which has been implanted by my Word.

The Sacred Seed

CHAPTER 4

The essential nucleus of your being, that seemingly elusive Christ center where my love and wisdom are stored, is far more available to the surface mind than has been previously realized. I erected no formidable partitions to keep human nature separated from divine nature. For this reason, the dividing barrier is unreal, it is non-existent, it appears to be there only because a form of mass-hypnosis is in effect which keeps my children believing that they are strictly human.

Let us return to the tomato seed and look at it more closely. Is it strictly a seed, a little collection of molecules that cling together in a certain way to form a certain kind of matter? If you had never seen a tomato seed, and had never heard of a tomato, the seed probably would appear to be no more than an insignificant bit of matter capable only of a short, unproductive existence followed by decay.

However, if someone told you about the tomato seed, explaining that within those apparently inactive molecules a divine pattern was held in waiting, eager to come forth, a pattern for a fragrant, leafy plant which would flower and bear delicious fruit, you would find it hard to believe. Knowing nothing at all about the reality of tomatoes, you probably could not visualize such an impossible thing as a big green plant with red fruit growing out of an uninteresting-looking seed. You would, no doubt, laugh uproariously at the quaint idea that all you had to do was bury it under the dirt, then keep it watered, and the forces of nature would co-operate with it to bring about its amazing change of form.

When you are told that your very being is a seed containing a pattern altogether as different from what you appear to be as the tomato seed-pattern is different from what it appears to be, this idea is just as difficult to visualize. You can accept the tomato idea readily enough because it is a very ordinary thing, with tomatoes you have seen it happen. But with human beings, the problem of visualizing a complete change of form is something else again, you have never personally known anyone to experience such a radical change. Human beings are born, they grow, they think and dream and create for a while, then die. If they contain a pattern for some other destiny, it is no more obvious to your surface mind than the pattern in a tomato seed is obvious to your naked eye.

Where is this Grand Cosmic pattern contained within you? Where is the nucleus of your own sacred seed? How can you feel its reality, believe in its existence, plant and tend and let it grow?

The nucleus of that sacred seed is your soul. Your soul is not an elusive entity hiding out somewhere within, your soul is the collectively organized life force in every atom, every molecule, every cell of your body. Your soul is the total consciousness of your being. It is the very awareness that animates you, that lets you experience living. Your soul is light, pure light, the very Light of Life.

Just as the plant pattern in the tomato seed is locked within its life force, awaiting proper conditions for automatic release, the Christ pattern within you is locked within your life force, awaiting proper conditions for a similar release.

In the case of the tomato, its life force is released when it is planted and kept moist long enough to interact with the forces of nature and draw unto itself the necessary building materials found in its surroundings.

In the case of yourself, the life force is released and begins to grow, drawing in the building materials supplied by nature, when your attitude of mind and heart provides the proper conditions for such growth. The needed growing materials are available to you just as they are to the tomato, they are supplied by me, and they would have been drawn unto you easily and naturally if your attitude had not caused conditions to be wrong for growth.

Your life force has, for the most part, gone unappreciated by your surface mind. You fully realized that you had a soul and that it was most likely an eternal soul which would, someday, have a chance to express more freely without the encumberance of a physical body.

Did you stop to wonder what the physical body was for, why I imprisoned your soul within one?

Did the tomato seed stop to wonder why its life force was imprisoned in the molecules of a seed? Did it look forward to the time when the seed would die of old age and set its life force free? No, it realized instead that it was in the seed for a purpose, that through the seed it could work its way to full maturity, to full fruition. It realized that within the seed its divine pattern was contained.

As man, you are a threefold being—mind, body, and soul. If either is missing, you are a seed without fertility. If the life force of a tomato is not within a seed, it cannot sprout and fulfill its destiny. If the life force of a man is without a body, it must clothe itself in the substance of a new body before it can fulfill its destiny. The soul is the sacred seed while the body is the vehicle through which it finds expression, in much the same way that the brain is the vehicle through which the mind expresses.

Your soul is a living part of me and my omni-present life. Your soul is constantly being regenerated and revitalized by the great life-essence which circulates throughout my cosmos. This life force reaches all, supplying animation to all, tying all things together in one dynamic wash of ever-flowing, ever-renewing consciousness.

This indescribable life force is being received by my children in varying degrees, depending entirely upon your attitudes. Your body is the vessel which receives it, your mind controls the angle of the vessel, and your heart determines how much of this River of Life you will let in.

The River is flowing all around you, in it you live and move and have your being. It is the supply found in nature from

which your sacred seed may draw to unfold within you the pattern of your
Grand Cosmic Self.

Your sacred seed, your spark of life,
awaits only the cooperation of your to-
tally-still heart center. When you have
extended this cooperation, the sacred
seed will begin to grow, to fulfill its cosmic pattern as the human hull falls away
and allows the holy metamorphosis to
be completed.

You have much to gain by learning to
appreciate your spark of life. Concentrate
on its presence, feel it, enjoy the silky
flow of it as it gushes up from the deep
well of your soul. This spark of life is
more than just the human consciousness
you thought yourself to be. This spark
of life is the very Light of Christ which
I wedded to you and from which you
cannot possibly be divorced. By simply
learning to appreciate it, you may cause
its flow to be enhanced until it gushes

up and becomes a living fountain that can never be diminished.

By the opposite attitude, you can decrease its flow. You can squeeze it out of your body altogether. But you cannot destroy it or cause yourself to become anything apart from the Light of Christ, for it is out of this very light that I have shaped your being.

The elemental nature of life is to increase, to seek more and more expression. This law of increase holds true within you as readily as it does in any aspect of nature. Life is a joyous, singing river ever surging onward. As you feel it and appreciate it, the little trickle finding outlet through your being will bubble up into a flood, drawing you into the beautiful pathway of the River of Life More Abundant.

This is what happens when you become the Living Christ. You do not suddenly become something else, or somebody else, you merely express a fullness of what you already are. You merely allow the Light of Life to come forward and increase. You merely allow the soul to stand forth in full reign over your body kingdom, your own personal soul whose right it is to have full reign.

Meditate on the life within you, cherish it. How joyous the surge of it! Imagine that surge doubled, tripled, multiplied by a hundred, by a thousand. That glorious Light of Life will respond to your appreciation and begin immediately to shine brighter.

It is a sad mistake to regard life as a bore which must be endured, with all its hardships, until death comes to set you free. Death is not the road to freedom, it will merely retard your progress. The life force in your body is the key to the freedom that you seek.

Take the old, familiar example of the caterpillar and the butterfly. If the caterpillar had been born, lived a while, then died, where would the butterfly be? The soul of the caterpillar is the sacred seed of the butterfly. The beautiful butterfly pattern is contained within the caterpillar even while it is a lowly worm, crawling on its belly.

In this case, I have predestined that the butterfly come forth. The caterpillar cooperates by instinct. It withdraws into its closet, its cocoon. A scientist has said that a "wave of determination" seems to start the process of metamorphosis on its way. Indeed it does! This wave of determination releases a hormone, an exciter, from a few tiny cells in the caterpillar's brain, these hormones stimulate the release of other hormones from the caterpillar's endocrine glands, and in the secrecy and silence of the little sealed cocoon a miracle of transmutation, of pattern fulfillment, begins to be accomplished.

When the brightly-colored butterfly emerges, it is an entirely different creature, free to fly about the earth in a dimension new to it. What has happened to the hull that fell away, that limited little worm?

With you, the fulfillment is not predestined. You may live and die time and time again before the truth about your sacred seed of life is consciously understood and subconsciously accepted.

When you do accept the Light of Life within you as being the route to a higher dimension, a "wave of determination" will be released in you and the needed alteration of attitude can be set in motion. Like the caterpillar, or the tomato seed, you will start to change. The wisdom of the soul, as it begins to assume command, knows every step that must be taken to transmute your physical body into quickened, refined substance.

This wisdom of the soul is me, your indwelling Father consciousness, doing the mighty works for you, rebuilding with the substances of life which are abundantly available in nature, in that everflowing River which fills the entire cosmos—my Holy Spirit.

The Holy Spirit

CHAPTER 5

As your Light of Life gushes into more expression, it will make you conscious of a Reality entirely overlooked by your limited surface mind. It will cause you to understand what your brother Jesus meant when he said, "The Comforter, which is the Holy Ghost, whom the Father will send in my name, he shall teach you all things, and bring all things to your remembrance, whatsoever I have said unto you."

This Comforter, or Holy Ghost, is also known as Holy Spirit. It is the ever-flowing River from which you can siphon life more abundant for yourself. I have made it available to each and every soul.

As soon as your reoriented surface mind sets up the right conditions, you shall be filled with the full measure of this Holy Spirit and it will open up for you the Doorway of a new dimension.

The process of receiving an increased supply of Holy Spirit and being renewed by it has been described as being born again.

You must be born again if you wish to enter the kingdom of heaven, or the new dimension. You must be born of the Spirit. Many of my children have sincerely tried to understand the meaning of an idea so mysterious as being born again, but it is seldom realized that being born again begins with a simple step which is no more than opening wide your mind and heart to receive a greater abundance of the life force which has animated you all along.

Your spark of life attracts the needed substance to increase itself in much the same way that the tomato seed attracts its needed substance or the caterpillar attracts materials with which to build. In each case, the original source for this life substance is the River of Holy Spirit, and each siphons from this source in accordance with its nature and its needs.

To ancient men, this River was known as the Holy Ghost, an invisible power which came down upon them from heaven, a gift which I bestowed after they had turned their attentions to me and had done everything within the limits of human strength to prepare the right conditions in their hearts.

Since my ways are eternal and unchangeable, it is just as possible now for men to be filled with the Holy Ghost as it was for men in days of old.

Not only is it just as possible, actually it is easier, for now you have the findings of science to verify the existence of this Holy Ghost, whereas in ancient times my invisible substance was ghostly indeed, and only a strong imagination, combined with even stronger faith, could accept the idea of its reality.

In the present day, a certain branch of scientific exploration is concentrating its efforts on the study of cosmic rays. Cosmic rays are detected coming from the depth of space, seemingly approaching from every direction, a great many of which are so highly energetic, so utterly unstoppable, they plunge in through the atmosphere and bombard the surface of the earth in fairly even distribution all around the globe. Similar cosmic rays, usually of lower energies, are continuously ejected from the sun and these fall in great quantities on my beautiful planet earth. The lower energy rays are often broken up by collision with atoms in the atmosphere, thus changing form into many different types of particles. The highest energy rays from deep in space are quite capable of plunging safely through to ground level, without collisions to break them up.

Within this superabundance of cosmic substances it is possible to find all the fundamental particles that go to make up atoms. If man had the technological know-how, he could "catch" these rays of Spirit and combine them into any kind of atoms necessary to make whatever substance he might want, whether that substance be animal, vegetable, or mineral.

It is these cosmic rays that have been called the mother element, my raw invisible substance, the force of life. They circulate like colossal rivers through all space, through all time. Their source is absolutely and eternally inexhaustible. I have filled the cosmos with this wonderful River of Life for the all-important purpose of keeping my beloved children supplied with everything they want or need.

If you believe in science, then you will surely believe in this rain of cosmic particles from the heavens, this ghostly invisible substance which is constantly penetrating everything on earth.

This mother element has been described as the Light that contains all and is all things to all men.

When you are born of the Spirit, you become conscious of the presence of this Light, you believe in it and in the reason for which it is sent. Your sacred seed of life can then attract it and incorporate the full measure of it without harm. Not only will it supply your every need, it will also be the source of your increased consciousness of life itself, the source of life more abundant, or the feeling of alive-ness greatly magnified.

Yes, as my Word tells you, when your

eye is single to my glory, your whole body shall be filled with Light.

It may seem incredible at first that your overworked, overweary physical body could be a recipient of this dynamic, on-rushing Light. Yet you would readily agree that your body is the temple of the Spirit. This is an idea you have always heard and accepted. Did you realize that Spirit would someday be discovered, studied, and slowly but surely understood? Also that the body, mysterious as it is, is releasing many secrets to the seeking techniques of science?

Before long, the full mystery of how the body and the great life force relates will be uncovered and proved. Exactly how the body is the temple of the Spirit will become accepted knowledge.

Your body was formed out of very sensitive Spirit substance, contrary to repeated ideas about it being formed from the dust of earth. Dust you never were.

You may become "dust" if you choose that road, of course, if you find it easier to believe in death than everlasting life. But you most certainly have a choice.

During the first few weeks of your life on earth, while you were no more than a tiny embryo of rapidly-multiplying cells, you were encased in a fluid-filled sac, a completely private world protected even from your mother's body. No blood from mother came in contact with your embryonic cells, no nerves connected you to her physical world. Not until you were approximately twelve weeks old did you begin to receive nourishment from her bloodstream through the placenta feeding station.

During those first twelve weeks without worldly nourishment, your rate of growth was tremendous, you were a very busy infant. By the time you were no larger than the head of a match, you had a brain, a mouth, the beginnings of

a jaw. Before the twelve weeks were up,
you had tiny arms and legs, bone, muscle,
blood, internal organs, and a heart already beating. Much further development and growth remained, to be sure,
but during those first twelve "foodless"
weeks your baby body outlined the cellular structure of a distinctly individual
person.

This miracle of "human" growth came
about because your sacred seed of life,
richly endowed with my wisdom, drew
from omnipresent Holy Spirit the delicate substance that it needed with which
to build a temple for itself.

As a result, you are living in a body
which my omniscience has constructed
with tender loving care, a body in which
I have carefully planted most precious
powers and gifts. These powers and gifts
have not diminished though seldom have
they been fully used. They abide in the
center of your submerged treasure chest,

available always to your lifted consciousness, your omniscient mind of Christ. To
your limited surface mind these powers
seem beyond the range of the possible,
but to me, your Father consciousness,
there is no limitation, no range of "possible" or "impossible".

Therefore, your ability to be filled
with, and use, the mother Light depends
entirely on the awakening of your submerged mind, it has nothing whatsoever
to do with "know-how" of your surface
mind. Does your surface mind know how
to use the oxygen which is taken into
your lungs? Does your surface mind know
how to receive vibrations of light and
color and transmute them into pictures
of the world around you that your eyes
behold?

No, your ability to transmute the Holy
Spirit is one of the sacred powers I gave
to abide in you. It is one of your most
precious powers, and it has been ne-

glected, ignored, unused, forgotten, lying dormant in the treasure chest of submerged mind.

As the great life force expresses itself, in you or anywhere in nature, its most essential action is taking place on the microcosmic level. The little things in life really are the things that make the difference. The activity that goes on in a realm invisible to your natural eyes is a very orderly perpetuation of chemical processes which make it possible for consciousness to experience. You are presently living in an organism which could properly be called a specialized chemical workshop. In this microcosmic world of cellular activity, the major work, being done at lightning-fast speed, is that of tearing down various molecular substances and synthesizing new kinds to fill the cellular needs.

The surface mind has no idea how this work is done. It is carried on below the level of awareness. It is directed by the wisdom of the soul. The orientation and condition of the surface mind, however, do play vitally important parts. They determine whether the body is a free and open outlet for the dynamic force of life, or whether only a trickle of this life force seeps through. A turbulent surface mind, oriented around the human self, is like a dam thrown up across a river, holding back its surging waters. But a quieted surface mind, oriented only toward my glory, is no longer the dam across the river but merely the banks through which the water flows.

This is why the Christ message teaches that you may be transformed by the renewal of your mind.

The full and varied use of my powers of transmutation begins to be manifested when your turbulence is stilled, when your mind and heart are quieted through your faith in me.

Not only is it your privilege to use these sacred powers of transmutation, it is your responsibility. It is your reason for being alive. It is the way my glory is revealed in you. It is the way you feed my sheep. It is the way you help your brother, not to show what you can do, but to show what *he* can do if he will learn to live the truth that Jesus taught.

If you can possibly believe these words, you will develop faith enough to hold your life in total stillness, and you will eventually see the truth of what I say with your own "human" eyes.

The reservoir of your heart will be converted into the Holy Grail, the glorious center that hungrily receives my Holy Spirit, magnifies it, and reflects it outward to a needy world.

You could already have accomplished the necessary change in attitude to make this possible if your surface mind had known the truth. But your concept of me has remained so vague that you had no reason for loving me with all your mind, heart, soul, and strength. You had no reason for keeping your mind's eye single to my glory, or Light. When you sincerely tried to love me, it was more like trying to love a "nothing" than a "something". Naturally, you turned back to earthly pastimes of a more tangible quality.

All the while, I am standing at the Door, knocking, knocking, knocking. My Spirit could give you life abundant if you would only let it in.

Nor will it destroy your physical body if you learn to hold yourself in total stillness and let the Light of Life already dwelling in your soul prepare your organism to receive an increase of this potent spiritual force. Your Light of Life will go to work throughout your temple, gently welling up as the fires of purification, and you will be washed clean of all evils and all negatives, with even the

very brain cells in which earthly beliefs
are stored being replaced with new cells
formed from untarnished cosmic elements.

Your body will become the burning
bush that is not consumed. It is true that
only the pure in heart, the pure in mind,
can receive a fullness of my Holy Spirit
without being consumed by it. But how
easy it is for your all-powerful Light of
Life to wash your sins away and trans-
form you into just this state of purity as
soon as you are willing!

In addition to being willing, it is necessary also to be quiet and believe, believe
so hard that belief turns into faith.

Faith always turns into experience, for
faith is more than just blind hope, it is
not an intangible emotion; it is a distinct
vibration which radiates outward from
you, into the mother element, and acts
in much the same manner as a magnet

to attract the forces of Spirit and focus them in your direction.

As the Holy Ghost descends upon you, it is received by a supersensitive area in the top of your head and drawn into your body temple where the wonder-working organs go about transmuting it into the building blocks of bodies and of worlds.

Please do not let this word picture of Holy Spirit cause you to think your Creator is no more than an infinite supply of pulsating atomic particles waiting to be used. Yes, I am just this, but I am so much more besides that it is absolutely impossible for you to conceive what I am from your present level of consciousness. Recognizing my presence as Holy Spirit is only a beginning point for your surface mind. This beginning point of recognition contains the power, of course, to exalt you to the Christ level of consciousness. As my Word promises, it is on this Christ level that you shall behold my face and come to know me as I Am.

The earth has recently been stunned by knowledge of the tremendous power contained within the atom. This violent splitting apart of atoms is an unfortunate example of the powers of which I speak. This is my spiritual power misused, or used in reverse, for I intended that man should utilize his talents to combine atoms, not to tear them apart. That which I have joined together, let no man put asunder!

The Second Birth

CHAPTER 6

Much has been learned about the physical endocrine system from the animal kingdom, even from the caterpillars. When hardly even a piece of skin or bone can be exchanged among my children without serious consequences, it is apparent that hormones of the endocrine system are of a very exclusive nature since some of them may be exchanged among species, human or animal, without harm, often with interesting results.

The endocrine glands manufacture, and secrete into the bloodstream, potent hormones that play a major role in regulating the chemistry of living matter. The amounts and types of these hormones make tremendous differences in the functions of the body. What happens to the caterpillar when its metamorphosis-hormone is released is a common fact of life. There is a certain kind of salamander, not so commonly heard about, which was injected with extracts from the human thyroid gland. This little salamander is a water-lover; normally it spends its entire lifetime living in the water. After being treated with the thyroid extract, it lost its gills and tail fin, developed air-breathing apparatus, and moved out of the water to live upon the land, a dimension new to it.

Endocrine hormones are life-giving, life-balancing, life-altering proteins. This is true in the case of animals just as it is in the case of men. At the moment, your endocrine glands are supervising the major chemical functions of your body, working in close cooperation with your mind. The glands are fully equipped to do more, much more than the mind has let them do.

As their primary function, the function of greatest importance, I intended that your glands should effect in you a more remarkable transformation than the caterpillar undergoes — changing you from mortal to immortal—just as soon as your "wave of determination" lets them know that you are willing.

If you develop the habit of hungering and thirsting after the Light of Christ within you, filling your temple with quietness harmonious to its flow, you will experience the momentous Second Birth, the birth of the Spirit. At this time, you will be on the road toward becoming perfect even as the Father in heaven is perfect. Your body will be caught up in the River of Life More Abundant; it can go on to full awaking, completing the development which was arrested as turbulent subconscious feelings began to work against your soul's natural growth.

Until the time of the Second Birth when your body becomes filled with Light, you are still numbered among the living dead. You are still counted in the herd of lost sheep headed toward the ditch of death. You are still chained to the cycles of the sub-creation and the painful road of evolving through sowing-and-reaping methods.

When my Holy Spirit is allowed to shine within, it will make you free at last by opening up all the important body centers and setting them off in the full swing of operation.

The first mission of the Spirit is to purify your surface mind, to erase belief in all appearances, to uplift your thinking and fill you with unshakable faith that the Door of Everything is waiting at the apex of your human consciousness.

The next mission of this beautiful working Light is to repair the substance of your cells, replace tired tissue, perfect damaged organs and renew "sick" areas, purify your bloodstream and keep it supplied with cellular food of the purest essence. The vibratory rate of each individual cell will be gradually quickened, or speeded up, by power contained in these rays of spiritual Light.

The great and glorious center of your heart will burst wide open, as if struck by a lightning flash, and you will become the vibration of Love, a vibration so exalted above the love of human emotion that the languages of earth do not contain words vivid enough to make the comparison.

This indescribable vibration of the heart spreads into every center of your sacred body temple, revealing to your astonished consciousness all the hidden jewels which were veiled to sight before.

The hidden jewel of the pineal gland, the mystical spiritual eye, will be made

known to you as it is stripped of its
"blindness" and resurrected to full activity. This precious spiritual center,
presently languishing in your submerged
treasure chest, is the all-seeing, all-know-
ing Eye of the Soul; it is fully aware of
all that I am.

When this submerged center is reawak-
ened, you will experience extended vision. The earth around you will suddenly
be illuminated by light more delicate,
more beautiful, more plentiful than the
light of the morning sun. These illuminating rays are a special kind of light
invisible to your human eyes. Unlike
sunlight, these special rays are never stopped by solid surfaces. They penetrate
everything, illuminating all the inner
parts, enhancing all the inner colors, revealing to your eyes a glory of the holy
ground beneath your feet such as you
have never dreamed. The walls of your
house will look transparent, the rock in

your garden will look more like a precious gem than like a stone.

You will be seeing a far wider range of the radiation spectrum, a joyous visual experience which limited human consciousness cannot possibly imagine. The "glass darkly" through which you had beheld the world before will not return to limit your vision again, for now the blind can see.

You are actually seeing the physical world by light contained within my Holy Spirit.

It is through the resurrection of the Eye of the Soul that you also become filled with knowledge. For in this same jewel is hidden the record of heaven, the truth of all things, the wisdom of the Christ.

When this center is fully active, you can do much to help your brother put his hand in mine, for you will be able instantly to evaluate his degree of receptivity and say exactly the words he needs to send him on his way.

You will be so fully conscious of me at this point that my still small voice will blend with your voice, and yours will be the Voice of God falling upon the earth.

The center of power within your throat will be fully awakened, and when your word rings out it will be alive with the unlimited creative force contained in Holy Spirit. If you should say "Lazarus, come forth," my cosmic substance would be motivated to respond, to fulfill the suggested pattern, the pattern of a rebuilt body temple for Lazarus; all this would be accomplished with the speed of thought.

If you should want to multiply the loaves and fishes, to turn water into wine, to complete the body structure of a baby born deformed, to return the old and broken to their youth, or any of a thousand other things needed to restore balance on my ailing planet earth, then you can do them all by the vibratory power contained within your spoken words. Indeed you will not need to speak at all, for the same vibratory power will be contained within your thoughts.

No longer will your words be empty and dried up. They will be backed and fortified with all my power to act, they will be living words.

You will be master of the elements as Jesus was, master of the atomic elements, master of the flesh, conqueror of all evil.

Evil cannot even get near you in this exalted state, for the electrified substance emitted as your body vibrates will rebalance any imperfection within the aura of your presence. The lepers in the crowd, or the cancer sufferers, will be automatically healed by your vibration as you pass by, without so much as a conscious thought on your part.

From the centers of your body you can

project a beam of radiant Light, which
to your extended vision will look as solid
as a rod of steel. On this beam you can
travel to any point in the cosmos where
your Father's business leads you. There
is no problem of survival in "vacuous"
outer space along the way. You are filled
with the Light-that-contains-all, and *all*
your needs are supplied by it.

I will literally light the way of your
feet, for the quickened vibration of your
body cells will cause a soft, exquisite radiance to emanate through the skin and
surround you. When you put your hand
in mine, truly you no longer walk in darkness.

You will be clothed by this Light,
clothed in heavenly white raiment, no
longer embarrassed by nakedness as the
human race has been embarrassed since
it fell from this Garden-of-Eden state
which all enjoyed together before satan
caused the separation by erecting the

blinding web of appearances, the sub-creation.

Satan is the independent surface mind, the human "self" that has decided it can rule the universe without me. Satan is the father of all evil, of all suffering, the author of death.

But your personal satan has been trampled beneath your feet, for now you are my ideal creation, my Grand Cosmic Being. You have been born again in Spirit. The power of this Spirit has opened up your submerged treasure chest and regenerated your mind, your heart, your body to full maturity, to wholeness of function. Those vital centers which served you with half measures before are now giving forth the full measures of their performance and perfection.

You have truly experienced the Second Birth, in the physical sense of the word as well as in the spiritual sense.

At the moment of your first birth,

when you were delivered from your
mother's womb and drew in the initial
breath of air, a marvelous unsealing took
place in your body temple. The lungs,
those two efficient bellows-like organs
which utilize the breath of life, had been
inbuilt to do this very work, but they lay
collapsed and dormant while you were in
the womb. The main bloodstream of your
body did not circulate through them, for
there was no reason why it should. It
could not be purified or oxygenated in
collapsed lungs that had no access to an
oxygen supply. In your immature infant
body there was another entrance to and
exit from the heart which your bloodstream unquestioningly followed. But at
the moment of birth, at the instant of
the first ingoing breath, the lungs were
suddenly unsealed, the blood rushed
eagerly in through channels that were
unused before, the alternate exit from the
heart was permanently locked—an amaz-

ing body organ which had apparently been useless began to serve its vital purpose.

At the time of your Second Birth, when the light of Holy Spirit is invited in to do its work, it will trigger other momentous unsealings of your body organs, just as the breath of air triggered the unsealing of your lungs.

This Second Birth will happen when you are thoroughly and utterly ready for my will to be done in you. This does not mean that you are ready to use me to bring these glorious things to pass; it means that you are ready to surrender completely to my will and let me use you for whatever purpose I decree.

In this state of complete surrender, your sustained prayer might be, "Thank you, Father, that I am blended with your Spirit."

As you continue to hunger and thirst for my presence, trusting your future to

my will, suddenly you will realize your
thirst is being quenched by the blood of
Christ, and your hunger is being satisfied by the body of the Christ. No longer
will you need to live by bread alone, for
you will find you are becoming my
Grand Cosmic Being of Pure Light.

The manna of Holy Spirit is the
"bread ye know not of" which Jesus
wanted to share with you. It is the mystic
union that makes you and the Father one.

You are now ready to do the works
that Jesus said you could do, and progress onward toward the greater works.

No longer do you approach me timid-
ly, hesitating to make demands of me.
Rather, you stand up courageously, full
of confidence, extending to me a vessel
as wide as imagination, and I keep filling it over and over with the Light-that-
contains-all. For now you know I am not
pleased when you are satisfied with a

little. I want you always and forever to ask a lot.

As you give and give and give of my Holy Spirit, you shall receive more and more and more.

PART TWO:

LIVING UPWARD

"Why sleepest thou, **O my Soul,**
And blessest not the Lord?
Sing a new song,
Unto God who is worthy to be praised.
Sing and be wakeful against his awaking,
For good is a psalm sung to God from
a glad heart."

—Psalms of Solomon

The Ascension Attitudes

CHAPTER 7

Why does your soul sleep, my beloved, leaving you in darkness? Why does it lie buried beneath your awareness like a treasure chest lying buried at the bottom of the sea? Why has the mind-that-knows-all in the center of your Being not broken through to the surface consciousness like Vesuvius erupting?

In truth, this is just exactly what the submerged mind is forever trying to do.

For centuries it has been saying to the weary surface mind, "He who loses his life for my sake shall find it." He who loses what he thinks he knows for the sake of integrating the mind in its Wholeness, will find truth more glorious than anything he has ever dreamed. He who loses his originality for the sake of slipping through the Door of Everything, will find originality beyond description. He who loses his leisure for the sake of studying the true Christ message, will gradually find himself no longer in bondage to the duties of the world. He who surrenders on bended knees, humble, empty, and hungry, will rediscover a long-lost fact.

The surface mind was never intended to be the center of consciousness. Rather, it is an avenue of awareness in much the same manner that the five senses are avenues of awareness. The eyes are the mechanism, but the mind does the seeing. The ears are the mechanism, but the mind does the hearing. The surface mind, in turn, is the mechanism, an avenue of contact with the world for the true center of consciousness deeper in your Being.

This true center of consciousness is so fully endowed with my wisdom that the surface mind and its limited knowledge cannot begin to comprehend it.

Knowing this, anyone on earth should be willing to relinquish the surface consciousness known as "self" for the sake of being reunited with the center of omniscience.

You know full well that a greater center of consciousness exists somewhere inside your body. But pretend for a moment that no such center does exist. Without it, you will need to take over the operation of your temple.

How will you direct your eyes to see? Does your surface mind know how to register an ordinary color? Take yellow, for example. Look at a yellow dress for one full second and during that brief interval the electrons in the retinas of your eyes will vibrate about five hundred trillion times. All the waves that have crashed upon all the ocean shores on earth during the last ten million years would not add up to more than that.

While this activity is going on there are several trillion other things you must get done at the same time. Every cell in your body is like a unique little universe carrying out its individual work. Yet all must coordinate with the organism as a whole. Can you control the most complex communication system ever conceived, your great nerve networks, without getting at least a few wires crossed? Can you think fast enough to receive and send uncountable numbers of messages in all directions at once? Might you not get so busy and so frustrated you would forget to take the oxygen from your lungs into the bloodstream and send the carbon dioxide out, or perhaps forget to beat your heart? Not to mention trillions of other things that must not be neglected for a second.

Can you think fast enough to direct the activities of your temple, or will you not bow down instead and wonder why you have been cheated? Why did your physical organism receive such a lightning-fast, one hundred-percent-efficient mind when your own surface mind is so inadequate the two can hardly be compared?

Yes, the surface mind is really not a mind at all. It is indeed a misplaced center of consciousness, and when you "lose your life for my sake", you find it because the center of consciousness then is able to shift back where it belongs.

If you could think fast enough to "work" your eyes, or any other organ in the body, you would not be thinking at all—you would be beyond the realm of thought, in the timeless realm of Being.

This is why the mind of Christ does not have to think, it just is.

This is why, down through history, as

my children worshipped signs and symbols, prophecies and predictions, leaders and advisers, no substitute was ever found which would satisfy the spiritual hunger. The gnawing hunger remained even when it was not identified as being the need for God. In all the universe, there is only one way to gratify this hunger—through the glory of the risen Christ, through integration of the surface mind with the omniscience of divine Being.

And there is only one place to begin this integration, right where your consciousness is centered at the moment, in your surface mind.

I am a God who requires understanding and your search for reunification with me is an individual responsibility Each must learn for himself how to live upward, as it were, through thought, into the realm of feeling, and then into the realm of Being.

This upward movement can begin just where you are if you relinquish the customary attitudes and fill your heart with a new song—a song of love, a song of praise, a song of gratitude.

Love, praise, and gratitude, arising from your heart center in silent expectancy, are the three Ascension Attitudes, those focussed attitudes of mind that exalt your feelings toward the Christhood level.

As you concentrate on these three attitudes—or one of them if there is one that seems more natural to you—making them a day to day, moment to moment, second to second habit, regardless of the unpleasant appearances which may be closing in around you, you will be learning to control the random mixtures of your thoughts. It is necessary, of course, to pull your random thoughts together and focus them on that Door in mind before you can ease through it. The three Ascension Attitudes supply the most important points of focus. They are your keys to the kingdom of true Being.

As you study the message of the Christ and begin thereby to get acquainted with Yourself, the potency of truth will light such a fire of enthusiasm inside you there will suddenly be a flood of reasons for your heart to sing out gladly.

And when your heart begins to sing, it will mean that you are reaching upward from the wheel of cause-and-consequence to put your hand in mine, giving birth to your "wave of determination", showing your willingness for my will to be done.

It will also mean that you are praying without ceasing, although you may not previously have thought of love, praise, or gratitude as being prayer.

Real prayer, in fact, has become a lost art in the modern age of worldly "wisdom". Its power has been discredited, it

has been regarded as the way for those
of low mentality, the method used by
weak-minded beginners, the last resort
of sinners. These beliefs regarding prayer
are prevalent in many minds in spite of
the fact that Jesus, with his enlightened
understanding, spent days and nights in
devout prayer, and saints throughout history elevated their consciousness to the
sainthood level on bended knees of prayer.

If you have never glimpsed the Door
of Everything, it is because you, too, have
lost the art of prayer. You have held that
Door in darkness, for if you had searched
for it by the light of prayer, it would
eventually have stood illumined before
your hungry gaze.

Contrary to racial belief, prayer is not
the words you hastily repeat under conditions of stress when I am suddenly re-
membered by your surface mind—prayer
is the intense, predominant attitude
which your mind and feelings have in-

dulged about the thing important to you.

If you pray quickly to me for help, without much feeling except perhaps that of desperation, then return to the former mental attitudes of fear and doubting, putting your strength behind these attitudes, which becomes your prayer? Which drops into the great subconscious reservoir, the quick plea for help or the predominant, steady attitudes to which your feelings cling?

If you will put forth the necessary effort to renew your steady attitudes by replacing them with the glad song, the lost art of prayer will be regained by you, and love, praise, and gratitude will become your way of life.

When I commanded you to love me with all your heart, mind, soul, and strength, I did so because this kind of attitude makes it possible to live upward toward the level of the Christ.

It has been hard for you to really love

me in the past, even when you tried sincerely, because it is not a function of the surface mind to manufacture love for God or love for fellowman. Truth is needed first, and when it is present there love will be also.

If you hold your mind on the good news of how you and I relate, how we complement each other, how we are inseparably One whether you are aware of it or not, you will no longer have to force yourself to love me by whipping up a storm of willpower and determination.

However, if you fail to hold your mind on this good news, if you hear it and forget it, continuing to think of me as a God afar off, in this attitude I will remain too nebulous, too remote for sincere love. Or if, perhaps, you return to the old habit of thinking I am a God of wrath waiting to impinge punishment at your first mistake, then fear of me will far outweigh your love. If you go back to thinking you cannot know me until after death, you are likely to wait until after death to feel anything about me at all, especially if you have been deceived into believing that your soul's future is secured through membership in some church. If you think I direct your activities through guiding spirits, you will idolize them instead of loving me as your guiding Father consciousness.

For these many reasons, understanding must come before genuine love for me. Understanding will fill your mind with a vision so beautiful, so desirable, so attainable, that you will never have to *try* to love me. Love will flood your mind and heart spontaneously every time you think of this great vision.

As you draw the vision to you, expanding it with all the detail you can gather — it will expand forever — the

Light of Christ within you will be growing brighter every day.

You cannot be "in this world but not of it" without first fulfilling the conditions that let you live upward until the threshold of that Door is crossed. And you cannot fulfill these conditions as long as you insist on worshipping duality, on worshipping the good and evil of the earth. It is necessary to give up your fear of evil, and your desire for earthly good, before you can become detached from this world enough to claim you are not "of it".

When you learn that all is perfection in the consciousness of the Christ, it is enough to make even the greatest good of earth lose its glitter by comparison.

With all your getting in this world, the truth is the most precious thing you could possess. My Word as taught by your friend Jesus, when properly understood and cherished, will set up such a strong vibration in your being that the vibration itself will make it possible to live this truth, and living it will make you free.

In view of this, loving me with all your heart, mind, soul and strength becomes a very natural thing to do. When you have really taken my star of truth into your heart, secreting it in the closet of your consciousness, you will be unable to stop loving me even if you tried. For, regardless of how often your surface mind may shout its doubts, your heart recognizes this familiar Word and your surface mind will eventually be put to shame.

The star of truth in your interior will glow zealously as you continue to feed it. And the great day will come when it flares up like a flaming supernova, blending with your Light of Life. At this time, the Word has been made flesh. One of the powers contained in your sunken treasure chest, the power to quicken and perfect, has been released and augmented by the Light of Holy Spirit.

Yes, go to whatever effort necessary to learn the message of the Christ, and after you have learned it you will realize that loving me is one of the easiest commandments that I ever gave.

Loving your neighbor as yourself will be easier then as well. For all your neighbors will become an inseparable part of the beautiful Christ vision which is blazing in your heart. No longer will you think of them as individuals cut out from different patterns, some dull-witted, others intelligent, some homely, others handsome, some greedy, others generous, some hateful, others loving. All will blend together in your vision, and you will know that all are really perfect because I am the Light of each one's Life. Whatever imperfection your brother or sister may be demonstrating in his actions is caused merely by his own false sense of being a lonely human who has to get along as best he can without me. Realizing this, you can forgive him for all his actions, for he knows not what he does.

This does not give you any right, however, to decide he needs converting and to try forcing his adoption of your opinions. Nor does it obligate you to listen to his opinions or change your ways to conform with what he expects from you.

It does leave you both free to go your own directions, to seek me by your own methods, or not to seek me at all.

Loving your neighbor as yourself has little to do with being eager to socialize much of the time, it has little to do with giving in to his dominance for the sake of human harmony, it has little to do with letting your time get wasted away while you indulge his idleness.

It has a lot to do with silently holding to your vision of the Christ in him without holding him responsible for acting in accordance with this high ideal. He may be filled with shortcomings, but you are to realize that someday they will all be healed when he decides to hunger for my Light. He will rise up from his humanhood like the legendary phoenix arising from its own dead ashes, and, as he soars beyond that Door, the years the locusts have eaten will be restored to him in full. For all the ages of lost wandering since he fell from the Garden of Eden, along with you, will be no more than a flicker on the timeless face of my eternal cosmos. All those chewed and eaten ages, with their accompanying pain and strain, will be forgotten in the true brotherhood of the resurrected Christ.

You are not likely to soar through the Door yourself if you have been weighted down with the belief that you must drag your neighbor along. Your responsibility to yourself and me is to keep your mind centered on the greatest good for all. Do not specialize among friends and relatives while so many of my beloved children the world over are in direst need of prayer. Expand your vision to impersonal consciousness and include them all.

None of my commandments are as hard to keep as has been thought if they are properly understood. I do not want you to exert force, or overpowering effort, in any one direction. This is not the method used by gentle, sweet, soft-spoken Spirit. Rather, I would have you literally relax into an awareness of my presence letting there be Light within while you contemplate the truth for all on earth. Then are you genuinely loving me and your neighbor as yourself.

The second Ascension Attitude which helps you live upward toward the realm of Being is the attitude of praise. It is so much like love as to be inseparable from it.

Praise me from whom all blessings

flow and as you do the all-important
Christ vibration will be stimulated in
your heart. Trying to make your mind a
vacuum and turn off all thoughts will do
little to help you live upward toward that
Door. There is no place in all my cosmos
for a vacuum, least of all in the minds
of men. Instead, I would have you focus
your thoughts on the exalted Christ level
and learn to hold them there until my
inner peace takes over.

Realize that all blessings do really flow
from me and it will help you fill your
heart with praise. Every piece of matter
you touch was once afloat in the infinite
sea of Holy Spirit. Do you not feel a
little awe that such miracles of transmutation could happen without cessa-
tion and yet pass by unnoticed? Think
again of that juicy red tomato as you
hold it in your hands. A year ago, before
the seed was planted, where were the
atoms now packed together into this de-

licious fruit? Were they not part of my invisible Holy Spirit?

No wonder Jesus advised you to consider the lilies of the field, how they grow. Do consider them for a moment. They toil not, neither do they spin. Nor do they worry about tomorrow. Their life force draws upon my raw invisible substance, never doubting, and how well they are clothed and fed.

Everywhere you look, if you are honestly seeking, you will find evidence of my omniscience working throughout nature. The basic structural pattern of all matter is enough to fill the surface mind with thoughts of praise and wonder. The atom, like a tiny, tiny solar system, is made up of a central nucleus, comparable to the sun, surrounded by one or more electrons orbiting in outer shells, comparable to the planets. There is a vast amount of space between the nucleus and the electrons; there is eternal motion of each and every part. That to-mato, then, which feels so solid to your touch, is more space than solidity, and never for a second are any of its internal elements at rest.

Everywhere you look, in nature or in fellowman, if you sincerely want to rise above the prosaic habit of taking every-thing for granted, if you sincerely want to feel inspired and stimulated to the quickened vibratory rate of praise, you will find factual evidence to feed your imagination.

My workings never cease, and there are more wonders right here on earth than this world dreams of, not to men-tion the myriad wonders of my heavenly realms.

I am truly in all and through all. You may watch me in actual expression if you will only open up your mind and take a thorough look.

The third Ascension Attitude embodying the vibration of the Christ is gratitude.

Once again, this attitude is so closely allied with love and praise as to be inseparable from them. When you have accepted the radiant Christ vision and allowed yourself to love it, when you have relaxed your intellect and learned to contemplate my omnipresence, then gratitude will be your natural reaction to it all.

As you contemplate the indescribable future awaiting each member of the human race as soon as he stands up to claim it, gratitude will well up in you automatically, flooding the reservoir of your heart. The vibration of gratitude is such a mighty creative force that it alone, if indulged continuously, could lift you free of the sub-creation more rapidly than you realize.

Begin to fill yourself with gratitude by contemplating your submerged mind and

its many hidden treasures. Give thanks
for that mind. Where would you be without it? It is the same mind that you will
use to do greater works than Jesus did.
It is the same mind, the same consciousness, through which you will experience
the indescribable wonders of my cosmos.
It is the same mind through which my
Light will flow into the body of your ailing brother so that he may be made
whole.

You have been living with this mind
for a long time. How often have you
stopped to marvel at its extensive talents
and feel gratitude that such a wonderful
endowment could be yours? Multiply this
gratitude and give reverent thanks for
all the minds of all the men on earth.

Think about your heart and its untir-
ing effort to keep your cells supplied with
the fluid of life. It is through this pres-
ently-opening center that the world-shak-
ing vibration of the Love of Christ will

soon be flowing. As you contemplate the nearness of such an eventful happening, you are entering the domain of mighty faith.

Give thanks for your senses and intensify them every one. It is through these senses that you enjoy my beloved world; it is through these blended senses you will go on to enjoy the crystal beauties of my many waiting mansions.

Give thanks for ten thousand other things beneficial to you every day which you may have been accustomed to taking for granted.

Then go one giant step further than you have gone before and give thanks for the things you want as if they had already come to pass. Look at the Grand Cosmic Being who stands out so sharply in your vision and give thanks that this holy personage is none other than yourself. He is yourself, he always has been, but since you have let him atrophy, give thanks you can undo the act and see him rise to life.

These three Ascension Attitudes are your perfectly-fitted keys, the keys to the Door of Everything. These keys are lovingly placed into your hands. You must use them persistently if you would see that Door fly open. For it can be unlocked only from your side.

Let some individualized aspect of these three Ascension Attitudes replace the stream of idle thinking that has been running through your mind, and your heart will be singing a glad prayer of contemplation, the kind of prayer that always brings results.

Never think of your problems or shortcomings as you fill your mind with prayer. Contemplating the problem lends the substance of your thought-power to it and makes it even more ferocious. In addition to that, the instant the thought of a problem comes into your prayer, your Christ elevation has been lost.

Let yourself contemplate only me and the treasures that are laid up in heaven for all my many children as soon as they unlock the Door.

As you weave these three Ascension Attitudes into the fabric of your daily life, you will be filled with great and mighty faith, for love, praise, and gratitude are major components of that essential attribute.

Take up your keys, my beloved Grand Cosmic Being, take up your keys, open wide the Door, and enter your natural habitat. Become the prodigal son who has returned to his father's house. All the hosts of heaven are waiting to welcome you home.

The Supporting Attitudes

CHAPTER 8

It will be most difficult to make love, praise, or gratitude a permanent quality if you fail to break the habit of judging by appearances. The problems and sorrows on the human level cannot be ignored as though they were non-existent. It is only by keeping your eye single to the glory of my presence, the glory lying underneath appearances, that you are able to become familiar with the "everlasting arms" of Holy Spirit.

All the while, the web of appearances may be there to contend with. But let your troubled heart be still in the midst of this great storm while the three Ascension Attitudes wake up your Father consciousness. The Father has dominion over any storm that rages.

If you keep looking at appearances and judging difficulties to be my will, it is the same as closing off the avenue through which I help you.

All appearances are abolished through increased understanding. When you accept the race belief regarding any situation, failing to hunger for that increased understanding, you have erected a dam across the flow of truth.

Great men of Biblical days were not the men who took things for what they appeared to be, they were the men who challenged appearances, the men who refused to accept a God that was anything less than perfect.

Job was not satisfied with the popular concepts of his day which taught that his troubles had come upon him because of sins. He was living under the earthly law, of course, and he had reaped what he had sown. Still, he had the courage to deny that I would make him suffer for a weakness I had given him, especially since he had done his best and was aware of no big sins. He hungered for a more reasonable explanation. Because of his hunger, a higher level of understanding was reached and his losses were regained.

Elijah found it hard to believe that his God could be a murderer. My sons and daughters by the millions have judged appearances and accepted death as being my will. Elijah rebelled most intensely, crying out in protest that I should even murder little children! The child that had died before him arose and lived again.

Even the disciples of Jesus were easily deceived by appearances. Before the crucifixion, he told them plainly that he was dying only to rise again. Yet when they witnessed his shameful death, they judged solely by what they saw and lost faith completely in his beautiful message of eternal life.

The hungry mind refuses to accept appearances; the obvious does not satisfy. A thousand religious authorities could preach their doctrines of good and evil and the truly hungry mind would listen and be hungrier than before.

The way my children finally come to experience truth is by standing up and challenging appearances, by throwing away the handed-down opinions and making room for an independent glimpse of my heavenly presence.

Seek and you will find has been the promise, but if you are not hungry, if you think you have already found, you will never reach your hand toward mine.

New wine cannot be poured into old bottles when the old bottles are already full. New truth cannot be poured into my children if they have been satisfied with an obvious God. If you accept the centuries-old idea that I made you with the capacity to sin, then leave you suffering because you have sinned, you are likely to go through life subservient to this hopeless situation, trying hard to be perfect but knowing all the time **perfection is** out of reach.

Perfection and truth are both acquired by filling your surface mind with emptiness, then hungering, asking, and continuously seeking signs of my all-healing presence. At first it may seem that you are getting nowhere, that all your yearning is being ignored, but this is just because it has been a long time since you tried to wake the Father consciousness, which, from the human point of view, is very deep in sleep.

Heaven is within you, of course, where it has always been, and when you reject appearances and begin to reach after its perfection, only then is it stirred up.

If Jesus had settled for appearances after Lazarus died, there would have been no momentous event such as a dead man's rising. After all, it had been four days, and Mary and Martha were quite certain, with decay of the flesh in process, that it was far too late.

Jesus always said, "Judge not."

Underneath appearances are the everlasting arms of the perfect world I created; judge only righteous judgment in accordance with this knowledge. Underneath the errant surface mind are the everlasting arms of your center of omniscience and perfection.

Signs of my inner heavenly kingdom do not precede your comprehension of this truth, they follow it. Signs do not precede your faith, they also follow that.

Exercise the best judgment that you can in contending with appearances, but let your thoughts and feelings continue to be focussed on the everlasting perfection which lies beneath the web of human sub-creation.

As you form these renewed mental habits, replacing worry and frustration with the glad song of the heart, you will at last be building on the mighty rock of faith.

The Mighty Rock

CHAPTER 9

The old earthly law of reaping what you sow can of itself be reapplied to help your consciousness rise upward. This law is saying plainly that if you sow tomato seeds you will reap ripe tomatoes; if you sow love, love will be yours to reap; if you sow belief in my perfection all around you, you will reap full familiarity with this perfection; if you plant a vision of your Grand Cosmic Self, your day of harvest will inevitably arrive. Since like always produces like, this is a law of infinite application, it works on every vibratory level, it cannot conceivably be broken. For thorns do not grow on thistles and neither do juicy red tomatoes grow on apple trees.

When you plant a prayer for bread I do not send a stone, and if you plant the seed of the Living Christ you will reap more than better humanhood. When you ask me, your Father consciousness, for the gifts of Holy Spirit, I do not send disappointment.

My gifts will flourish so bountifully your heart will burst into a song of praise much like the one that Clement sang so many years ago: "How blessed and wonderful, beloved, are the gifts of God. Life in immortality! Brightness in righteousness! Truth in full assurance! Faith in confidence! Temperance in holiness! And all this has God subjected to our understandings."

You have the capacity to believe as Clement did that I have truly made you perfect and placed you in a perfect world, and this perfection is yours, subjected to your understanding. Subjected to your willingness to believe. Subjected to your faith.

Anyone can believe in happenings he has seen take place. Anyone can believe in events being reported in daily coverage of the news. Anyone can believe in new inventions or great scientific discoveries —after they have been proved. Anyone can believe in the obvious God when the "impossible" perfection has been left out.

If you use faith only to bring about things you know can happen, then you are in for a wonderful discovery when you put faith on the job to bring about things beyond the range of human reason. This range beyond is really the home of faith, the realm in which faith works.

Until enough faith is exercised to rise like incense into this range beyond, you will be unable to transcend your human level. Until you recognize that my methods are truly above the understandings of men, you simply will not stir up the mind in you which was also in Christ Jesus. For Jesus not only had faith in my impossible methods, he had such great and mighty faith his desires became experience with the speed of thought.

Faith, needless to say, is a very dynamic vibration. It is the combined vibration of the mighty Ascension Attitudes. It is one with the vibration of my Holy Spirit. Therefore, when faith is set in motion, it makes possible the everlasting affinity between your soul and my Light.

You have used faith many times. You have used faith in troubles to bring upon yourself the things you feared. You may have used faith in poverty to keep yourself in want. You have used faith in limitation to hold your talents back. You have used faith in physical breakdown and old age to destroy the reality of your life force, the reality of eternal youth.

You have used faith in short lifetimes to keep yourself in bondage to the cycles of birth, childhood, old age, death; rebirth, childhood, old age, death.

Since faith has been used so many times to bring destruction upon yourself, you have already practiced using great and mighty faith. Now all you need to do is reverse your attitude and lend your faith to me, using it to invite the unfoldment of the sacred pattern which is trapped within your soul.

Rebuilding your attitude upon the rock of faith causes it to become a firm foundation beneath your feet which is absolutely immovable. Once you thoroughly understand that the ways of the Father consciousness are impossible to the surface minds of men, your faith cannot be shaken by anyone alive; it would be easier for the doubting Thomas to shake the earth itself than move this firm foundation on which your feet are placed.

A miracle is merely a manifestation, in the earth realm, of perfection that exists already in the timeless realm of Being. Miracles could be happening every day among my children if all lived upward toward the Christhood level, refusing to be held back by false belief. The average human consciousness is so bogged down, however, beneath the pressures of daily living, it takes an emotional intensification of some sort to boost it upward even a slight degree. Faith itself cannot be exercised on such a low, nonhungry level, except to bring more human good or evil.

Exercising great and mighty faith means looking inward toward the Christ, not outward at the darkness.

Jesus himself confronted many he could not help because of their nonhungry attitudes. The surface minds of these lost souls were so completely closed to truth not even a glimmer could penetrate. Those who already had their "gods" sneered and persecuted. Others came to worship him because he seemed to have some superhuman personal power. Not many comprehended the truth he was revealing well enough to apply it for themselves.

If you want to be lifted off the wheel of cause-and-consequence, you must learn truth and then believe it until it is demonstrated by my Spirit.

Belief is the partial opening of your heart center, and when it is not present your heart is completely closed.

Faith is far more than belief. Faith means the heart has opened wide, it is radiating its dynamic vibration, it is ready to be filled with Light.

Belief widens into faith when nourished, cherished, and practiced. Faith turns into experienced knowing.

The point stressed most in all the Master's teachings was that you must believe.

The greatest deterrent to your ability to live upward is doubt, that unstable, wavering attitude that positively keeps your heart from running over. What happens to the water in a reservoir when its bottom is full of holes? You are a reservoir for my living waters, but if you are full of doubts, they are the same as holes, my waters leak straight through.

Belief itself should be applied to things beyond the range of what seems possible. For if you can bring yourself to the high point of belief, faith as a grain of mustard seed is sure to follow. It is a fact that a little bit of faith can reach a long, long way. And a little bit of belief can stimulate that little bit of faith.

Appearances say hard times are always just around the corner. Expect them and be prepared.

The still small voice of your indwelling Father consciousness says perfection is waiting for you everywhere. Turn to me with faith and let me reveal it to you.

As you plant belief in the everlasting arms, your weary surface mind will reap eternal rest. Though you may chant for all the world to hear that you believe in God, if you deny that my realm of perfect Being is for all on earth to enjoy, here, now, and forever, you are indeed denying me. Your belief is falling short of what I expect from you. You are ignoring my word of truth.

My good has been prepared for eons without number; it is revealed before your eyes in accordance with your faith. When you begin to live upward toward the Christhood level, you will cease the habit of exercising faith in failure, faith in poverty, faith in trouble, and adopt the habit of singing praises for my gifts. Subjected to your glad heart's singing, these precious gifts may be experienced. My power within is greater than any seeming-power without, as you must know by now. My power within can deliver you from the most violent storm that ever raged. This power within waits only to be applied through the channel of your faith.

You always demonstrate on the level where your consciousness abides. It is not necessary, as a result, for you to learn the secret of how to demonstrate, how to bring the invisible into form, because you have been doing this all your life. The power of mind cannot do otherwise than demonstrate in accordance with the way in which it is used.

Therefore, you do not need to exercise faith in your ability to perform miracles, for if you will only exercise enough faith to lift your consciousness to a higher level, the miracles will take care of themselves. They will happen not as a result of human thinking, but as a spontaneous result of Christlike being. You could not stop the miracles any easier than you could stop your life.

As you learn to put me first, to have one goal and only one—that of living upward toward the level where my will can be done in you—all outer conditions will naturally resolve themselves, not because you are trying to change them, but just because you *are*.

If you have been trying to heal a disease or defect in your physical body, forget these efforts and be at peace. Ignore such appearances as best you can and lie back singing in the everlasting arms. The healing will come spontaneously as your consciousness floats upward to touch the edge of mine.

Come unto me in this manner, all you who labor and are heavily laden, and I will give you rest.

On the higher levels of consciousness it takes no mental strain to recognize that imperfection is nothing but the subcreated web held before my Light.

Only by the use of great and mighty faith can you direct your mind toward me and learn to hold it there. The limited race beliefs, as you took part in them, were self-inflicted crosses which you should not have had to bear. You can throw these crosses to the winds, standing up at last to see my kingdom without the "glass darkly" before your eyes.

When you have unwavering faith that the mind in you is omniscient and that it is truly one with the mind of the Christ, you will find yourself living under the freedom of my grace. Be wakeful always against the awaking of this inner mind.

When you have faith in all the promises I have made to you, you will be established on the mighty rock, the firm foundation that cannot be moved. Your soul will then stand forth from the center of your being, to reign over the body temple as Lord of Lords and King of Kings. This is the kind of faith that quickly grows into the long-sought state of conscious knowing.

There is, of course, an indescribable difference between knowing me and just knowing about me, as you will shortly realize if you continue efforts to live upward.

Faith that you can be One with me is the very magnetism which will draw you through the Door of Everything and let you know me fully.

The Total Stillness

CHAPTER 10

My Holy Spirit comes upon you to lift you through that Door in mind after you have reached a state of total stillness. This means retiring into the closet of your consciousness where you worship me in secret until I reward you openly.

Your efforts to live upward must be accomplished in the privacy of this closet, in quietness and in confidence. The flame of enthusiasm which truth has lighted in you was not intended to be dissipated in idle talk, in efforts to reform your relatives and friends, or in attempts to teach the great Christ message. This flame of enthusiasm is a precious fire of mine, the fires of purification,

and it is there to do its purifying work
in you as you nourish, cherish, and feed
it in the silence. My fire is not there to
make you feel so spiritual you redirect
your enthusiasm, in the name of service,
to interfering with the religious beliefs
of your brothers. The only person you
are responsible for changing is yourself.

It shows a complete lack of humility
if you catch a glimpse of truth and, without waiting to digest it or understand it
clearly, set out to spread it everywhere,
hoping one and all will bow before your
knowledge. Do not let yourself be deceived into becoming such a false teacher.
Your falseness will be recognized, because truth half learned still tends to
stay within the range of human reason,
mixing good and evil, justifying its false
god, the god who was not God enough to
create perfect children.

You do not want to be another of
these blind leaders running in the same

big circle as the herd, thinking you are someone special because you have a private rut.

Authentic teachers of my truth must have enough humility to lean completely on my strength and stay within their closet until I open up the door.

Nor can you reach a state of total stillness where mighty faith takes over if others all around you are promoting their false gods of imperfection. Evict these noises from the privacy of your closet and listen only to the words of those who have discovered the one God of perfect Being.

False teachers everywhere will be humbled by their own misdeeds until eventually all will know of the perfect world I made, and the perfect children whom I love so dearly I am waiting eagerly to take each one into my everlasting arms. The radiant energy of my Spirit shows no partiality, it rains through one and all, it waits to exalt the blackest sinner alongside the whitest saint as soon as there is surrender in the heart.

It is never wise to compare personal notes about the steps of your development or try to impress anyone by bragging about your spiritual accomplishments or intuitive powers. This urge to gratify your ego will not reveal your spiritual side at all; it will be only a sure sign of how far removed you are from the required state of humble stillness.

Surrender in this humble stillness is the final step toward making possible the lightning flash which I will send to set you free.

Your troubled heart cannot be still at all unless you believe, without any reservation, that I am a Father who forgives only. Even the failings of your surface mind are not enough to keep my all-powerful Spirit from lifting you through the Door to freedom.

As you study and believe, pray and

meditate, major strides are being taken toward removing all old fears and quieting the turbulence in the reservoir of your heart. When this turbulence is quieted, you will be transformed into a state of perfect peace. For the peace that passes understanding is one of the many treasures buried in your submerged mind. It can easily be released and mirrored throughout your entire temple.

When you learn to touch this peacefulness, going back to it in meditation every time you have a chance, gradually it will become a part of surface mind and you can enjoy its presence night and day. As more and more it is released from the deep well of your soul, you will reach the high level of consciousness where nothing can ruffle the serenity of your being.

It is in this total stillness that you can at last be guided by my still small inner voice.

This inner voice is vibration from your Father consciousness, the wisdom center of your Grand Cosmic Self. For this reason, it does not speak to you with words to be heard by your ears, it is a voice to be felt, a vibration as sweet and unmistakable as the music of the spheres.

The fact that my voice must be felt, not heard, may seem disappointing at first if you have occasionally tried to feel my inner guidance and been unable to separate it from the confusion of the self. This difficulty has arisen because you have not treated the mind and body as one, and because negative emotions have dulled your state of consciousness, thereby dulling your receptivity to the delicately-refined vibrations of the Spirit.

Here is another reason for the total stillness. With repeated, faith-filled practice, you can resharpen your sensitivity to the point where my voice really does vibrate in your surface mind like a beautiful note of music, ringing loud and clear, leaving not a single doubt that you have heard its message with unmistakable accuracy.

Regardless of the extent to which noise from the surface mind is interfering with your ability to "hear" your still small voice, this loving Father-Mother voice is always trying to rescue you from difficult situations with its all-encompassing knowledge.

Just as your body is able to be fully cognizant of many things at once, through the complexities of the senses, so your submerged mind, with its unlimited capacity, is fully cognizant of all the seen and unseen, the hidden and the obvious, the future and the past, and it can lend this full awareness to you with a speed incredible to mortal consciousness.

This inner wisdom-center is your personal Secret Place, the Secret Place of the Most High, and if you want to become fully conscious of it, abiding in the shadow of its almighty protection, you need only to be still—very, very, very still—and practice the long-lost art of "listening".

Practice is the answer to anything that seems difficult, as you know so well. The painter would never learn his skill if he did not practice. The swimmer may become a champion, but not without continued practice. The carpenter's house may not be perfect if it is the first one he has built. Even the farmer with his tomato patch may grow more luscious fruit after he has gained the experience offered by the first attempts.

When you tried previously to receive my inner guidance, did you listen once or twice, perhaps without much hope, and then give up in doubt? If so, practice is the answer, sustained, sincere practice which can become a delightful habit in almost no time at all.

Many changes will be apparent in you as this habit is established. You will notice a great renewal of mental activity, a clarity and quickening of your ability to think, a keenness of good judgment, an enhancing of imagination. These changes will be inner changes; your outer activity will decrease while your inner activity increases.

You will find yourself slipping into a rapturous inebriation with real thinking, effortless thinking of original thoughts, not just a rehashing of old ideas that have accumulated in your mind. This inebriation with effortless thinking has been experienced by a few creative or inventive persons to a small degree. It could be experienced by everyone to a degree beyond belief.

Be forever willing to reject guidance from outer sources and listen in the total stillness to your own small voice. It is your one true personal guide in every situation.

If you cannot quiet your ruffled feelings enough to be still and listen, while you practice you might pray for me to help you. Think of the beautiful peace that passes understanding and let your prayer be one of trying to comprehend this inner peace. You may be a long way from experiencing it, but regardless of how turbulent you feel, you can offer up this turbulence on the altar of your heart, and hold your mind upon the inner heavenly kingdom until peace begins to crowd the turbulence out.

By the same token, if you are not sure it is my voice you hear when you are in the silence, prayer will liberate you from this confusion too. You can pray to know my voice, and as you do your sensitivity will be heightened until you are quite familiar with this beautiful Light of Wisdom.

You will soon understand that your still small voice has two aspects to its nature—it redirects you when you wander just as reliably as it intoxicates you with its guidance.

As the voice of your re-director, you recognize it as conscience. Since you have felt the sting of conscience, it is obvious that your still small voice is easier to hear than you may have thought. There is no denying that conscience is a penetrating vibration, that it originates beyond the reaches of the stubborn surface mind, and that it can "whip" you with greater severity than your earthly father whipped you even in his angriest mood.

Nor does it leave you guessing as to what it says. You always know why your conscience "hurts", do you not?

The voice of conscience is not a dictator to which you must feel enslaved. It is a tender, guiding friend. It is holding you by the hand while you learn to walk with me. If you miss a single foot-step, it pulls your hand, as it were, to guide you back onto the narrow razor's edge.

You need only to turn to it, to trust, obey and love it, and your receptivity will increase until you never have to doubt that my wisdom, indeed, is guiding you infallibly. Conscience does not condemn you for the mistakes you make, it merely helps you find the way again. Give thanks for this masterful Light of Wisdom from the mind of me and watch its value to you grow.

In its other aspect as intuition, the still small voice can lure you upward like the sweetest beckoning song. Here again, as you realize that intuition is your Father-Mother mind in communi-cation with you, your sensitivity to it will be greatly heightened.

This aspect of your still small voice may not be as easily heard, however, as the stinging voice of conscience. You may need to be so totally still that you can hear your own cells singing before the vibration of intuition, with its embodied message, can be clearly heard by you.

Be very still and practice listening. Ask me anything you want to know, then wait in quietness and carefully watch your thoughts. Do not strain or make an effort, just sit in silence and let my coherent Light play across the weary brain-cells of your surface mind.

From the depths of this total stillness, the voice of intuition will spring up like a musical note and you will hear its message as unmistakably, as understandably, as the message from your conscience. Not only will it lure you into more creative thinking, it will be your source of truth, and you will know what you believe, and what you want to do, without knowing how you know it.

With the help of intuition, the surface

self will come to realize what a hopeless task it undertook in trying to manage the affairs of life without omniscient mind. It should then be delighted to surrender to my will.

When the self is ready to admit its folly, its utter helplessness to do one single thing without me, the level of consciousness is being reached wherein reunification can take place. As long as that misplaced center of awareness wants to be the "brain", I do not subdue it with force or violence. But when it is quiet long enough to hear the intuitive voice of truth and seek marriage with the Father consciousness, the mystic union will take place.

"I can of mine own self do nothing" becomes the attitude of the surface mind which gives up efforts to glorify itself and invites the Christ within to use it— instead of it trying to use the Christ. "Not my will but Thine be done."

Stillness truly can be total stillness as the mind lets go and "waits upon the Lord" before that Door.

The day will come when the Door is opened and its threshold is repeatedly crossed. Sometimes the footing may be upset by a tinge of doubts, an absence of humility, or an outburst of the self which forgets it has surrendered. But this high-level footing can be regained through quietness, faith, and confidence.

The human self, tottering like an infant at that mighty Door, completely surrendered to my will, is ready for my lightning flash.

The Lightning Flash

CHAPTER 11

"As the lightning that lights out of the one part under heaven and shines unto the other part under heaven, so shall also the son of man be in his day." What your friend Jesus meant when he said this was that the earth of your body will be lit up from end to end by my Light, even as swiftly as the lightning moves from one end of the sky to the other, when your day has come.

I steal upon you like a flash in your consciousness and you know not during which hour to expect me. When I do come, lo! I come quickly—and your reward is with me.

The bars of iron that kept you a prisoner of the sub-creation melt before my burning flame, and you look through that widened Door inside yourself, feasting your hungry eyes upon my heavenly kingdom. Yes, at last you know you really were the Door of Everything! The film of unbelief that separated your surface mind from your submerged mind is torn asunder, and never again will you be entangled like a helpless fly in the web of sub-creation.

"Receive ye the Holy Spirit," Jesus said, and if you continue to believe that even you with all your failings can receive it, since I love one and all, you shall be changed in the twinkling of an eye from mortality to immortality.

And you shall know with full realization that I am indeed a God of Love and Light through whom the superimposed imperfection of the sub-creation will be erased.

The last and greatest evil to be removed from my precious planet earth is satan's evil, death. Death never has been and never will be the way I call my children home. The fact that Jesus taught that death is an evil to be overcome has too long been ignored.

Your greatest teacher did not utter a single word unworthy of attention. You must not continue to ignore his highest, most "unreasonable" teachings if you want to apply his truth enough to demonstrate it for yourself. The vision drawn by him is workable and attainable to the surface mind once it is understood.

Meditate on the things he said regarding the subjects of death and life. One of these things was this: "Verily, verily, I say unto you, if a man keep my word he shall never see death."

Could any talk be plainer?

It is true that life is everlasting regardless of how many times the body dies. It is true that the soul lives on and creates a new body for itself. But it is also true that the soul is endowed with wisdom, it knows death of the body is out of harmony with my universal law of Life.

This is why death has such a morbid connotation to my earthbound children. Your soul knows it is the way of earth-believers. It yearns to be exalted by the vibration of the Ascension Attitudes so it can travel the way of saints. In order to travel this high way, it needs a body which overcomes the destructive earth vibrations and is transmuted into Light.

Death is the way of separation, it is not the way of Oneness. Although death may, on rare occasions, be painless and easy for its victims, it is never painless and easy for the loved ones left behind. This is because I created all my children to be together in love, together in Spirit, not separated by unknown universal vastness. Though you were able to roam the cosmos when you knew it as the Garden of Eden, you were also able to be bodily in the presence of a loved one, whenever your heart desired, with the speed of thought. Death is contrary to this perfect law of non-separation which all exercised most freely before the foundations of the earth were ever laid.

Death not only leaves you physically out of touch, it leaves you mentally out of touch. It is most assuredly the sorrowful road of separation. And I would never have penalized any of my beloved children by setting them on this road of pain. Death came into existence along with all the unhappy experiences, as a result of your misthinking.

It will go out of existence as each one learns to surrender the limited self to me. Death will be destroyed by truth.

Many have suffered mental torture because of the barbaric belief that sinners who die are punished forever in eternal lakes of fire. This misinterpretation of the

Bible teachings must be relinquished from your consciousness before you can reach the all-important state of total stillness.

The hell-fire symbology was a way of saying that the surface mind does indeed sear and singe with self-inflicted torture as long as it continues to plant belief in mixtures of good and evil. Hell, therefore, is within you just as surely as is heaven. Hell is the realm of the independent surface mind, the level in consciousness on which all dwell before discovering, and entering, the Door of Everything. Hell is on your side of that Door, heaven is on my side of it.

When death does come, it releases the weight of gravity and temporarily frees the soul from earth. But it does not change the vibration of consciousness from the human level. There is no escape from the vibration of yourself except by practiced change of thoughts and feelings.

Nor does death cause the released consciousness to go directly to celestial levels. Consciousness, when departing from the body, automatically seeks its own level of vibration among the levels of the psychic realms, which are comparable in understanding to the levels of the earth itself.

The psychic realms are still a part of the web of sub-creation, for this is where disembodied souls await their chance to take on new bodies and thus come back to earth for another lifetime, another opportunity to fulfill the beautiful law of Life, the law which puts an end to the monotonous life-death cycles.

Consciousness changes slowly as you will notice by observation of yourself and others. This is true when the consciousness is incarnate or discarnate. A consciousness does not automatically come into greater understanding of my truth just because it has left the body. Sometimes it can be taught. At other times, it may be just as closed to new ideas as it was on earth. If the sacred seed of Life was understood in psychic realms, there would be no need for these between-lifetime areas, for all souls therein would be winging forward into celestial brightness. Unfortunately, these many souls are tied to earth by binding emotional chains that draw them back again. They come refreshed, renewed, and rested, with eager childlike minds which can be shaped by truth if they resist the world's misteachings. Every lifetime is a new beginning, a new opportunity to be annointed with Light and rise above the trap of death.

Indeed, every day in every lifetime is a new beginning.

If you want to see the Christ fulfilled in you, take hold of the message of the Christ, love it, expand it, *live* it, pray that I may confirm it to your surface mind.

You will receive my confirmation, clearly and unmistakably, as the Light of Christ begins to glow in you and becomes a new, warm, comforting inner presence. You will know beyond all doubt that I am with you all the way.

Then as you learn to put me first above all things and surrender without the slightest reservation to my will, your Light of Christ will be increasing every minute of every day. You will be like the tomato, steadily growing to maturity on the vine.

The moment will come when you, like the tomato, have reached a perfect state of ripeness. You are ready to be "picked".

This is when, as Jesus said it, you will be as the lightning that lights out of the one part under heaven and shines unto the other part under heaven. In other words, by the time your surface mind becomes conscious of it, your whole body is already filled with Light, and the veil that separates your surface mind from the unlimited realm inside the Door is rent asunder as swiftly as a lightning flash.

The truth has made you free and you are free indeed!

Many of my children have yearned to do the works of God without being willing to purify their minds and become worthy of these works. Others have believed they were already pure, refusing to admit their own bad habits. But all have sinned and fallen short of my glory. Each must give up his self-glorifying habits, or pray to be delivered from them, before the brightness of the Christ can be revealed for all the world to see. Each must take up my rod of truth and live it in every word and act before my lightning flash can strike. Each must repent and be transformed by the renewal of his mind.

If you keep my commandments then am I bound, but if you keep not my commandments then you have no promise.

Put on the great Ascension Attitudes and wear them like a robe of light. Through the practice of these attitudes your mind can be renewed, your heart can be made pure. Through the practice of these attitudes, you can be led into firsthand exploration of my many, many mysteries.

"Who is able to interpret the wonders of the Lord?" sang the writer of the Odes. "For he who could interpret would be dissolved and would become that which is interpreted."

You, too, may be dissolved, as quickly as a lightning flash, and become the Light of Christ which you are learning to interpret through my wonderful word of truth.

"For he that is joined to Him that is immortal, will also himself become immortal."

The Door of Everything

CHAPTER 12

A Door is set before you and the keys have been presented with which it may be opened.

My still small voice is there to guide you, to comfort and encourage you, to lead you by the hand.

Faith is your magnetic force and prayer illuminates the way.

Rejection of all limited race beliefs keeps you from being weighted down with false ideas you have outgrown.

Refusal to judge by appearances keeps you from losing faith in my omnipresent perfect Being.

Enthusiasm sets alight in you the fires of purification.

The total stillness conserves your vitality and lets it quicken the vibration of your consciousness and spiritualize the chemistry of your cells.

Surrender indicates humility and willingness to lean upon my wisdom and my strength.

My lightning flash will let you know when the Second Birth has taken place.

Walk with me straight through that Door and watch in exultation as your humanness is dissolved. When this has happened, you will glance backward and discover that the "Door" never did exist at all—it was only a false belief which had become a part of you, the erroneous old belief that you were separated from your Creator. The Door was not put there by me, you erected it yourself, therefore it was unreal. It does not matter now, however, for you are inside my heavenly kingdom where Everything awaits you.

Everything is not many things, it is One.

Everything is Love.

Love. Love as you have never known it or imagined it to be. Love, the only true force in all creation, the Light out of which all things were made, the cohesive power which holds all things together. Love. The very Love of God which I have promised would be shed forth through the hearts of men. Love, concentrated beyond measure in the River of Life More Abundant. Love, the most indescribable, all-inclusive vibration in existence.

Love contains all the purified qualities of mind and heart even as white contains all the colors of the spectrum.

Love contains Everything.

Just as there is no real dividing barrier between your human self and your Grand Cosmic Self, there is no real dividing barrier between your human love and your Christ Love. Christ Love is human love multiplied by a thousandfold, ten thousandfold, ten million.

Human love is limited but Christ Love is infinite.

Human love can be polluted, it can become selfish and possessive, it seeks to receive as well as give, it can be counterfeited or pretended.

Christ Love is always pure, it cannot be touched by human ways, it is impossible to pretend it. Christ Love changes every receptive thing it touches from imperfection to perfection. It seeks nothing for Itself.

This great Love of God is the reward for all who overcome the mixed thought habits of the earth. It is the reward I promise to bring with me as I lead you through that unreal Door. It is the new name I will write upon your forehead. It is your complete fulfillment of the Light-that-contains-all.

For Life is Light and Light is Love.

Your soul is the vessel which must receive this Love, your little human self would be consumed by it. Let your soul stand forth and LIVE. For of what profit is it if a man gains the whole world and loses his own soul?

Come!

Meet me just inside the Door of Everything, in my timeless realm of Being, where all the perfect qualities of your Grand Cosmic Self will intersect and blend into one precious jewel—the precious jewel of Love.